The
Pyramid
Theory
of Marriage

The Pyramid Theory of Marriage

Tony Gulvin

First published in the United Kingdom in 2009
by Argot Publishing

ISBN 978-0-9561420-0-9

Produced by
The Choir Press
www.thechoirpress.co.uk

Contents

To my unborn

Preface

The devil is a notorious poisoner. It is said that his larder contains but few condiments that cannot taint or sour anything these ingredients touch. Perhaps this is why the truly sickening display of early morning pseudo-liberal propaganda, thinly disguised as populist chat shows can only cause a genuine sense of nausea. Indeed, pundits, in the form of Trisha, Jeremy Kyle and Matthew Wright, actively compete with each other for public revulsion. Unsurprisingly then, from the opening credits, an ever reactionary Wright (host to channel five's "brightest" broadcast), performs his drunken clown routine in order to both manipulate and distort the "facts" he has force fed an unsavoury panel of sycophants to regurgitate. Furthermore, once their saliva drools, these pronouncements are held up to an incarcerated studio audience as meaty insights worthy of digestion. There are even occasions when his programme sinks to the lowest levels of café culture, in the sense of encouraging Muslim panelists to speak against alcohol, stuffed- blouse feminists to censure science – as and when it suits them – and his daily "guests" to belch out any tripe imaginable. On matters as weighty as the disintegration of marriage, or the ignorance often underpinning so-called received wisdoms bequeathed by our forebears, his viewers must, however, feel starved to their stomachs.

Yet gut-churning spectacles such as these cannot satisfy our English appetite for serious communal debate. After all, we inherited from our ancestors a taste for free and reflective conversation at every ethical strata; a tradition which has survived both an intrusive Church as well as an increasingly paternalistic government. This is why Tony Gulvin's welcome contribution to such discussions genuinely nourishes like a veritable banquet. As a moral observer, his arguments are strikingly clear and founded on classic notions of liberty and consequence. He also regards every man, woman and child as entitled to a uniquely fulfilling destiny, unhampered by defunct concepts of pointless restraint. He uses the notion of liberty therefore, in at least two senses: first, as the metaphysical capacity to make decisions without the coercive influences of others, while the second meaning may be understood as a tacit political perception that "Everymans" individuality is innate and worthy of respect for its own sake. In this, Gulvin is certainly amongst recent English, French and American thinkers who have vociferously upheld both of these definitions; although Gulvin seems afraid that they have become dangerously confused in our age.

Coupled with his identification of the Romantic State and his call for a profoundly rational approach to contemporary relationships, Gulvin serves up a series of intellectual delicacies to his readers, while overtly warning them of the price they must inevitably pay for indulging emotional inauthenticity. Moreover, he darkly contends that such a bill can only leave a bitter flavour in the mouth when considering the desperate plight of the unborn. New life is not, he indirectly stresses, a commodity, which can be bought or sold in the dreary market place of sexual deceit, but remains a miracle entrusted to spiritually responsible partners. A social reflection that can only be applauded.

David Parry
London, September 2008

Introduction

There is something intrinsically arrogant in believing what one says and thinks to actually be true. Humility dictates that truth must come from others, yet since we are all 'others' to other people, it is our duty in the interests of knowledge to make our observations and opinions as credible as possible.

Aversion to the views of others, it is worth remembering, is just as potent an indicator of truth as is adherence or qualified admiration. Any one of the three, however, only has merit when our reaction to the 'truth of others' is respectful. Respect involves consideration, contemplation and honesty; prejudice does not. So in the spirit of RG Ingersol, whose turn of the twentieth century book *On the Liberty of Man* asked its readership to give their prejudices the 'night off' I, too, ask any response to the following to be born of the mind and not the knee.

With this essay a mere three paragraphs old it has already used the concept of "Truth" four times. In a sense this does and does not matter. It matters because, on one level, I want to attack everyday assumptions by appealing to the concept of eternal truth, or more to point, the potential lack of it. On the other hand my basic argument relies for the most part on the application of common sense notions of truth.

Truth as a concept has hitherto had the greatest minds, past and present, locked in philosophical dialogue. A debate, though perhaps thoroughly intriguing, is mainly limited to academic circles and largely ignored by the average person, in which I include politicians, judges, police and other such decision makers. Furthermore, it is a debate given a very wide birth by various moral lobbyists. Certainly, I would argue, most of us tend to see the truth bereft of its historical and cultural baggage. Hence, comments such as "well it's true, isn't it?" are far more prevalent than "well it's true if one holds the universal transcendental a priori metaphysical foundations to be correct". Let's face it, most people, when asked what houses are made of say bricks and do not worry what bricks are made of. The point being then, whilst my argument is essentially a practical one, it also draws on an ideal of honesty and in doing so, is more immersed in virtue than pragmatism.

To avoid confusion I want now to explain a little further the nature of my position. The purpose being: to dispel any lingering accusations that might be held by the reader when reading. Firstly and most importantly, I believe children want two parents, especially when children have been initially exposed to such a situation. The argument that it is better battling parents separate rather than expose youngsters to the constant bitterness and disharmony only has real value under the present set up of the institution of marriage and long-term relationships. This is not to say that I do not sympathize with the sentiment per se, but under the Pyramid Theory of Marriage it becomes less important. The dilemma of whether or not to stay together in the "best interests of the kids" is not simply a sad fact of life. It is a pragmatic response to the ill thought out assumptions and expectations on which our relationships are based under the current system. In short, this theory is designed to produce happier couples in the first place thus reducing the necessity to separate in order to save children from the burden of dysfunctional family units.

Secondly, marriage, as I define it, centres on the emotional bond between two people as opposed to any legal bond. So, my definition of 'marriage' as I shall use the term in this book is: any long-term, day-to-day, sexual relationship based on the mutual idea of foreseeable continuation. In saying this, obviously there are some practical implications of being legally bound. However, attention to these nuances between the two states will only serve to fudge the fundamental issues that dog the modern relationship. Suffice it to say the behavioral habits of, say, a couple who have been married for eight years and a couple who have been going out with each other for eight years is not qualitatively different. Essentially, we all expect (or at least want) to be held, cherished, fussed over when unwell and monogamy in the vast majority of cases is not only expected but seen as a pre-requisite of continuation.

Thirdly, I believe the assumption that the family unit is essential to the fabric of a free society to be correct, and something most of us instinctively feel. However, given the exponential rise in divorce rates it is clear that mere appeals to traditional values have had, and will continue to have, little or no effect in stemming let alone reversing present trends. Indeed, the family as presently organised will only worsen and the negative implications for society as a whole can only be guessed at.

Fourthly, this is written by a heterosexual and is aimed

at heterosexuals. However, no intolerance of gay and lesbian culture should be inferred. It is merely outside the intended parameters of this argument. After all, plenty of gay and lesbian literature does not feel the necessity to include the heterosexual, or as a gay friend of mine calls us, the 'breeding' community. Nonetheless, some of what I argue has been influenced to an extent by my observation of the gay community's approach to relationships. That said, whilst this is not a book about gay couples parenting, if through my aim to defend the longevity of heterosexual relationships its message transcends other possibilities of family organisation then all well and good.

Fifthly, the Pyramid Theory of Marriage is based on the assumption of genuine desire by both participants to make their relationship last. Therefore, whilst endorsing plurality and diversity, in many ways my argument is a very conservative one albeit somewhat liberal in its means of achieving its goal. It is definitely not an apology for monogamy. However, nor does it advocate (I choose the word carefully) the 'free love' mentality that came to fruition in the sixties.

I also feel it necessary to point out that any personal experience which I bring to this essay is done so on a purely anecdotal level. To extrapolate solely from one's own experience on to the rest of humanity, would be ridiculously pretentious. In addition the path outlined in the following text is in no way due to an overnight sea change of thought born of hurt or bitterness. It is the culmination of many years of thought and observation, which in turn has produced a refreshing and liberating honesty I find absent in the love affair with monogamy.

Finally, any references to philosophers are, to all intents and purposes, coat hangers for my argument. Therefore, if my interpretation of their thoughts are de-contextualised in a sense it does not matter, for their role is mainly an organisational one in helping provide a framework for what I want to argue. They also play the cosmetic role of an 'academic fig-leaf' hopefully lending a certain modesty to what is, after all, just an opinion.

The Pyramid Theory of Marriage was completed in June 2000 and has had minor recent amendments for publication. By the way, for those wanting to know why the metaphor of pyramid is in the title, it is because it was part of an illustrative story in the original text which, unfortunately, didn't make it into the final draft, and which outlined the idea of a long lasting relationship as a true wonder of the world.

Chapter 1

Happiness

'If there be some one thing which alone is a final end, this thing will be the good which we are seeking.'

(Aristotle)

'Happiness above all else appears to be absolutely final in this sense, since we always choose it for its own sake and never as a means for something else.'

(Aristotle)

The Greek philosopher Aristotle stated that the supreme 'good', lies in something final. He believed that the collective results of all our actions are in search of some final goal. That final goal roughly translates as happiness, which Aristotle considered to be 'time honoured and perfect' as 'all other actions are done for its sake'. Simply then, happiness is not merely a rung on the ladder of life it is the very purpose or point of the ladder in the first place.

However, Aristotle tells us that in order for the collective consequences of our actions to lead us to the state of happiness those actions in themselves need to be born of goodness and should be continually, not just occasionally, applied. Being good when it suits one is not sufficient to achieve the supreme goal of happiness.

Essentially there are two basic ideas here. Firstly, everything we do is done so in the pursuit of happiness. Secondly, what we do must be in accordance with two further criteria, namely goodness and longevity.

This is the basic model I want to use to open up my discussion. However, before doing so, I feel it is worth reiterating this is not about accepting or not accepting my reading of Aristotle or indeed accepting Aristotle's overall ethical philosophy. I simply want to adopt his essential idea because it appears to me to coincide very much with our general understanding of what long-term relationships should be all about. I believe most people want their relationships to be fundamentally happy, long standing and based on an imperative of goodness or love. Therefore, I want to argue firstly, that marriage is an action done in the pursuit of happiness. Then using the second theme, I want to move on to explore the present apparent inability of marriage to be fundamentally anything more than a phase in one's life rather than a long standing, happy and 'good' relationship.

Marriage and happiness

If all actions are part of a collective set of actions in the pursuit of a final goal then, in terms of significance, I suggest that a solid relationship is arguably the single most important thing we do in our striving for happiness. So much so, it could be seen as the key to a genuine and sustained accumulation of happiness. Good marriages are the 'hand-rails' of our ladder to happiness; the rest of our lives are the 'rungs'. Or, changing metaphors, relationships help themselves to a greedy slice of the happiness pie. Success of any sort tastes better shared. Other contributions we might make will always be dulled if they are achieved alone. Put another way: prolonged involuntary single life is like being permanently hungry. Whatever you are doing you would prefer to stop and eat before continuing.

Relationships preoccupy us. Obviously some prefer their own company, but the vast majority, do not. Who is going out with whom? Who fancies whom? Whose marriage is doing what? Who has split up and who has not? Who is having an affair with whom? These are not major sources of conversation for no reason. Many of us have sat in the pub opposite friends whose deep and meaningful relationship has recently come to an end. Cheerful Charlies they are not. The sense of "nothing else matters" indelibly etched in their features, their conversation if they offer any, is sporadic and predictable. They stare blankly with an enormous wrench in the pit of their stomach. The cold sense of suddenly being alone is hard to put into words but we have nearly all felt it at some point in our lives. Unfortunately, separation is like death, in that no one can face it for you and the emotion you experience is genuine grief. Arguably, the situation is harder than dealing with a death (initially at any rate) in that there is a sense of it doesn't "have to be", and of course one's sense of grief is compounded by a sense of rejection. Time, however, will in most cases heal the death of love and often with hindsight it may even be viewed quite positively. Obviously, relatives who have lost love ones are never afforded such a luxury.

In saying this, lost loves, missed romantic opportunities haunt a memory and can be a major source of regret. In short, we care about relationships. They matter. So, we should, and do, have long-term relationships because we want to be happy. But in order to be happy our relationships have to be successful. However, the term successful marriage is at present misused. A successful marriage is generally deemed so if it is seen as one that survives the test of time and in doing so provides a relatively stable environment within which children are raised. Although I would accept this is politically preferable to separation in terms of its social and economic ramifications, the resigned pragmatism of the parents paints a pretty bleak picture as far as our final goal is concerned. In short, people will stay together unhappy and it is perfectly possible to have a 'successful' relationship devoid of genuine happiness.

Plainly, given the unprecedented rise in divorce rates and taking into consideration the 'divorces' of those not legally bound that can never be known, [modern marriage] is falling well short of any such criteria. Simply, relationships based on long term commitment are displaying an ever-increasing inability to last. Moreover, I want to argue that it is this very inability to pass the longevity test that signals the end for the paradigm of marriage premised on romantic idealism. Paradoxically, I further contend the sense of idealism is in fact little more than pragmatism in disguise and it is this somewhat false idealism that we should be addressing, replacing it with quite literally "Romantic Idealism". However, this is a point that will be discussed in chapter two and developed in chapters three and four.

The thrust of my argument for the moment, is this; the long lasting, yet not very happy marriage is respected (and rightly so) against a backdrop of relationships faltering at an ever-increasing and some would say, alarming rate. However, if relationships are seen as more of a necessary sacrifice, partly, in the name of children and if I am right in my assertion that people *do* form serious bonds in respect of an intuitive drive towards happiness, there is obviously going to be tension between the two. A tension palpably far too great for many couples because we must assume separating is also done in just such a pursuit. We look for new partners in the name of happiness.

Our first idea is that all actions are done with our ultimate happiness in mind and marriage, I argue, is the biggest single contribution the average person makes to his or her collective effort to realise ultimate happiness. However, the rhetorical landscape that surrounds marriage is one of sacrifice, compromise and if we are honest, boredom. My argument is that the compromise and boredom are for the most part, a direct consequence of the sacrifice most seem to take for granted as part and parcel of married life. That sacrifice being essentially monogamy in that it effectively endorses and underpins the abstract notion of Relationship which having predominance over the individuals concerned, leads to inauthentic, unfulfilled lives. However, again for the present, this is a notion I shall only touch on as it is more appropriately dealt with later.

For now, I am simply suggesting that happiness or personal inner contentment is a thing that has been forgotten or certainly down played where the public conception of what it *means* to be married is concerned. In the sense that whilst marriage or Relationship may be a conscious decision by an individual in the pursuit of his or her own happiness, what they enter into and agree to do has been essentially shaped by public opinion in an historical and cultural sense. And in this chapter I want to silhouette the negative contribution the rule or pact of fidelity plays in the 'forgetting' of happiness. The trap we have set ourselves always catches us, in that symptoms start to appear as "facts of life" or reality... "just the way it is". Yet, we have created a new truth only because we all believe it. In other words "it's just the way it is" perhaps because it is "the way it is", precisely because of what we agree to do in the first place. For example, if I agree to do a job for too little money, on a one-off basis it will not make much difference. However, if I continue to do so eventually my whole standard of living drops. Now if I forget that the fee I agreed in the first instance was too low, I will probably begrudgingly accept my relatively unhappy economic circumstances as "just the way it is".

Therefore, I propose that for a marriage to be deemed successful or truly authentic longevity, goodness and *happiness* must be present. This is so because happiness, not children, is ultimately the purpose of relationships. If children were the purpose, and we are not like animals solely at the mercy of pre-determined natural forces, why do people leave their kids if not in search of a situation more agreeable? Bereft of happiness, and more recently convention, marriage as both an institution and an 'idea' will obviously be more fragile. Debatably, the only adhesive ingredient left for long-term relationships is the mediocrity of security. And that could be said of a prison in that the institutionalised prisoner afraid of impending freedom is something we understand but do not feel comfortable with. The prisoner may have company, food and shelter but most looking in on a situation like this and hypothetically putting his or her shoes on, would like to think they would embrace such an opportunity and make the most of it. Marriage, for security alone is not trying to win, but merely trying not to lose.

Happiness and the Good

The above proposition brings into play the second theme in our 'Quasi-Aristotelian' model. (The first, being marriage is an action that is pursued in the quest for happiness). The second tier to our initial assumption is that genuine happiness is achieved by acting in accordance with 'complete goodness' (Aristotle's words). Remember here I am only accepting this model within the confines of long term sexual relationships and adopting it so, because of its broad appeal to everyday common sense.

So what is the good? And how do we go about enacting it?

Aristotle identified acting in accordance with the 'good', as observing a 'mean' between excess and deficiency. Very briefly, the idea is this: too little generosity is a bad thing as is too much generosity. Bluntly speaking, being 'tight fisted' does not meet the imperative of the 'good' just as being so generous that you cannot afford to feed yourself or your family does not. The point of virtue is situated at the point of just the right amount or 'mean'. This idea can be seen (loosely applied) in the maxim "everything in moderation", which, again, has a useful everyday common sense message. However, certain actions or emotions are simply bad in themselves so cannot *have* a 'mean'. Murder, stealing and envy to name but a few 'imply evil'. Just the right amount of murder does not come into it.

So, the median point is the point of virtue, but how do we find this happy medium? Aristotle's answer lies in his belief that the human being is intrinsically, a rational agent and, therefore, we are enabled to establish the point of virtue through our powers of reason.

To find a 'mean', or more loosely to act in moderation, requires a large chunk of self-control. And self-control is guided by reason. In addition, self-control also embodies the concept of sacrifice, which, must then also be guided by reason. Therefore, for sacrifice to be virtuous, or, in line with the 'Good' it must have a rational underpinning, certainly in the context of average day to day life. (The irrationality of a one-off piece of altruism or, indeed, extreme selfishness in a life or death situation is not particularly relevant to our discussion). So, the role of sacrifice with regard to happiness can only have virtue if it is based in rationality. It must then follow that sacrifice bereft of a *rationale* has to contradict our sense of reason and, therefore, must impinge upon the goal of life, namely happiness.

For example imagine this ...
A " Oh those roast potatoes were delicious, are there any more?"
B " Well, yeah there is, but Paul will be back in a minute and he's got to eat."
A "Oh, right, ok don't worry about it then."

Compared to ...
A "Oh those roast potatoes were delicious, are there any more?"
B " er, yeah"
A " great, can I have a couple?"
B " er.. no."
A " Why not?"
B "er ... because you ... you ... shouldn't"
A "What do you mean, I shouldn't?"

B " Well ... you just shouldn't, I just think it's better if you
   don't"
A "Right ..."

The simple point being unexplained or non-rational sacrifice contradicts the human sense of justice, virtue, right and
wrong. Instinctively we need a reason.

   Thus, the question we should be asking, or the problem
we should be identifying, is what the nature of marital
sacrifice is? And does that sacrifice contradict our sense of
reason? If it does, then addressing that could pave the
way for happier couples, which, one would naturally
have to assume, would be less disposed to separating.

   The most sensible way to answer this question is to
examine why people split up. The main reason for failure
will be the most honest indicator of the sacrifice asked of
us. Obviously, there is no single reason. However, anthropologist Laura Betzig in her study of a 160 societies states
that infidelity is the most common reason for divorce. I
do not think we need professional research in order to
enlighten us on this one; a quick survey asking people
what they thought was the biggest single reason why
couples separated would be enough to demonstrate that
statistics do no more than officially confirm what everybody already knows. However, the BBC reported in 2005
that extra-marital affairs were the number one reason
with 27%. Interestingly, in the same report it stated that
13% of divorces were down to one or other partner
suffering from a mid-life crisis. What does a mid-life
crisis entail more than trying to re-capture one's youth
resulting in attempting to make ourselves more attractive
to anybody but our partner? The other reasons cited are
physical abuse, emotional abuse, substance abuse,

economics, and family strains. Nonetheless, infidelity is the biggest single justification. In addition, it could be argued that if all hitherto undetected infidelities simultaneously came to light, divorce would suffer a rather sudden increase. In which case infidelity's less covert competitors of economic difficulties, physical abuse, emotional abuse and substance abuse could possibly appear mere "also rans". In the same vein, there are no figures for couples who have stayed together but whose relationships have been inherently damaged by adultery. And, of course, there is no official knowledge as to the number of common law relationships that have terminated due to 'extra marital activity'. Just as there is no way of knowing the role of denial, diplomacy and so on in cases of separation, where those involved cite reasons other than infidelity.

At this juncture, I ought to defend my assumption that infidelity is a *cause* of separation and not a *symptom* and, in turn, an accurate indication of sacrifice. My answer is, simply, that if it is a symptom of other problems, why aren't the real causes cited as grounds for divorce? The point is that infidelity is acceptable grounds purely because of the notion that fidelity and marriage go 'hand-in-hand'. People say that sleeping with someone else is, in the end, symptomatic of deeper problems. I would say that those deeper problems are in actual fact symptomatic of monogamy. I do not doubt for one minute that it is possible for an individual to 'reluctantly' stray in a secondary way. By this, I mean in response to a partner's disagreeable actions and not primarily in the sense they deliberately instigate the situation. So, for example, persistent coldness or distant behaviour from a lover may result in the need to look elsewhere for affection. However true this might be it ignores why our partner is cold or distant in the first place. Perhaps they simply are unhappy in the confines of a monogamous relationship. Monogamy, as a foundation to a relationship, necessarily creates an environment that in turn creates our excuses as to the 'real' reasons that lie beneath our inability to remain happily faithful. However, this is a point that I will develop in chapters three and four. Suffice it to say, I feel it is far safer to accept adultery at face value. Put another way, if a third of a country died through starvation, I would not try to put the real cause down to them not liking the food that was on offer. I would accept famine as the more likely cause. Taking the analogy one step further, if it was agreed at the outset not to irrigate the land or plant any crops, I would not try to offer the fact that people did not like feeding on leaves and insects as the underlying cause of the disaster.

I have now argued that monogamy, or more correctly the lack of it, causes more divorces than anything else (bearing in mind that I am using divorce in the broad sense of separation in general). I now want to go further and try to show how the self-control or sacrifice required to be monogamous is nowadays in direct conflict (possibly at a sub conscious level) with Reason, and therefore in direct conflict with our unwritten, but doubtless, goal of happiness. However, before doing so I want to make it clear that in no way do I believe marriages of yesteryear were fundamentally much different. According to Bertrand Russell, the notion of a marriage based on romantic love was first conceived in the late eighteenth century, and only gained 'taken for granted' status in the nineteenth century. And it is from this period onwards that my comments as to the nature of change in relationships are confined.

Relationships have been swimming in the sea of sacrifice and compromise more or less parallel to the shore. The only difference, for the modern couple, in the context of durability, being that the tide has gone and we are standing in the mud. In other words, circumstantial change has left our basic disposition all too exposed and therefore the disparity between self-control and Reason and thus happiness, has simply become too onerous a task to contemplate realistically.

Circumstantial change

Obviously, there is no single reason as to why we are unfaithful in practice. The anthropologist, Fisher's book *The Anatomy of Love* informs us there is no such thing as a naturally 'life-long' monogamous society and there has never been one. In addition, the myth of the seven-year itch is in fact far closer to four. Whilst I agree that an average practical response to our natural disposition is probably around the four-year mark, I reckon that most of us start mentally much earlier. I hear the male reader sigh in agreement and the female reader broadly speaking far less convinced. However, I believe women, if they are honest, have the fundamental urge to stray just as much as men. This area of disagreement I want to delay discussing at this stage. However, I will say that anthropological studies of societies where the 'one rule for men' and 'one rule for women' does not apply, have shown there is no difference in the 'adulterous' sexual behavior between males or females. Indeed, according to Bertrand Russell, in casting the female in the role of the temptress, organised religion is at root, the culprit for the 'lad' and 'tart' disparity.

The point then is that it is a brave person who seriously suggests that naturally we only want to have sex with one person for life. The normal defense of the one on one scenario is that 'civilized' moral behavior based in Reason, facilitates self-control in these matters for the sake of love. However, as I see it, the self-control has to all intents and purposes lost its rational underpinning due to circumstantial change and, thus, the prevailing environment no longer has the power to check the human condition. The disposition of man has not changed since the beginning of time where sexual urges are concerned. It is the environment that has changed which not only has produced more infidelity but also a far more negative response (in terms of separation) to what undoubtedly always went on. Rather like what happens in John Wyndam's *Day of the Triffids*. The Triffids (being man-killing plants) were always there, posing a lethal threat to the humans but the humans could contain them because the killer plants moved extremely slowly and people could see them. It was only when the circumstances changed and everybody, bar a lucky few, went blind that the real threat to human society occurred.

So what are the changes which make the task of being faithful far harder in the present day? I think there are six main areas of change to discuss and whilst not exhaustive, represent the most important potential developments. These (six) are the longevity of life, the decline of religion, contraception, the proliferation of real choice, the invention of unreal choice and, most importantly, the emancipation of women. Naturally, these developments have had many ramifications for all areas of human experience but, again, I am only interested here in the affect they have had on monogamy as a choice.

Before taking each area individually, I feel it worth noting this is an opinion and, therefore, speculative by nature. In that spirit the following is merely touching on areas that could be, and almost certainly have been, investigated and documented at some length. Therefore, I do not apologise for their brevity; I merely want to get across what seems to me basic areas of change which common sense deems bound to affect behavioral aspects of relationships and, therefore, in the same vein statistics are seen as of little relevance. After all, if I am at a football match I do not need a tannoy announcement stating that the attendance is 56,386, to know there are a lot of people there.

Longevity

Hardly any Sherlock Holmes points for this one. The more time you give something the greater the chance of it happening. Even allowing for a comparatively greater infant mortality rate, the average life expectancy is without doubt greater for the average working person certainly since 1900. Therefore, broadly speaking, a marriage is expected to last in some cases up to twenty or so years longer. Yet the rule governing the hardest task of all has been denied any sort of modification. Not surprisingly, the longer the exposure to temptation, inevitably, resistance decreases. It could be argued that a person's defences can also be strengthened over time but this seems to me an argument supported by the actions of the pre-sixties generations and in no way suggests those generations were particularly happy to oblige the dictates of moral opinion.

Contraception

This point, is self explanatory, hence there is no need to say more than simply there are bound to be 'more takers' when the negative consequences once associated with doing something beautiful, pleasurable and exiting, have been removed.

The Decline of 'Religion'

Religion or namely Christianity traditionally taught celibacy, Paul of Tarsus certainly advocated it in his letters to the Corinthians. Nonetheless, if marriage was embarked upon the Christian message, as traditionally interpreted by religious leaders, enforced a monogamous culture on its adherents with the threat of eternal damnation always hovering in the background. Obviously, growing up constantly under a cloud of fear is bound to affect attitudes and behaviour. A believer who was tempted to stray faced the dilemma of the potential terrorist 'grass', always looking over his shoulder and never quite comfortable with the inevitable dodgy fate not far around the corner. The difference of course being that God was more likely to accept an apology and a promise of non-repetition, than the average terrorist or Mafia boss. Nevertheless, with such indoctrination side-lined by a general disbelief another preventative hurdle has effectively been removed.

Increase of Choice

I have split the increased choice argument into two categories, basically making a distinction between *real* choice and *unreal* choice. Nonetheless, both represent a genuine proliferation of perceived choice and have played no minor role in undermining our mental security and overall sense of contentment with the 'norm'.

We have all had the grandparents over for Christmas. Everybody is seated at the dinner table a large plateful in front of them and as sure as "I could do that" at a modern art gallery, one of them will say "I don't know where to start". This is a very simple example of choice causing a dilemma even if the sentence is probably more of a courtesy tool. Remember television before the video? There was a real problem when you wanted to watch two programs that clashed. We did not like the sacrifice, recognised the problem and invented the video recorder. The point being choice creates the desire for both and eventually they clash leaving us dissatisfied. Nietzsche summed up the fact that choice equals sacrifice or what economists call "opportunity cost", with the phrase 'by doing we forgo'. Nonetheless, merely being a fact of life does not make it any easier to choose and the more choice the harder it is to be satisfied with any choice.

Real Choice

Without doubt we live in an age where choice has never been more prevalent. Capitalism is after all premised on choice. Free market economics is all about choice.

Also, against a backdrop of increased population, choice has also spiraled on an emotional level. Technology in both mobility and communications has taken us in a little more than a century from the horse and cart to the high performance car and the aeroplane, and from the telegram to international telephone links and now of course the internet (the Fortino group claim one third of divorce litigation is caused by on-line affairs. Relate cite the *Friends Reunited* web site as having equally had a considerably disruptive influence, as many people, unhappy with people they no longer "love", seek out old flames).

The result of this transport and communications revolution is twofold. Firstly, greater anonymity and, secondly, we simply meet more people. Obviously, the two are interrelated in that we meet more people within a wider anonymous context and with the privacy of anonymity greater infidelity is much more likely.

It would be foolish to pretend that there are only a few 'likely suitors' for any individual. It is our very individuality that makes this false. The individual, by nature, is as diverse and complex as it gets, and set in a context of relative freedom there are bound to be many points of commonality. These, added to basic sexual chemistry, mean it is perfectly possible (albeit not socially acceptable) for a plurality of emotional bonds to be formed. Indeed, the strange thing about monogamy and what it stands for is that it brings guilt to the plurality of emotional and sexual connections, despite it being a perfectly natural phenomenon. Guilt, as things presently stand, arguably has the ability to censor the emotional bonding between a 'forbidden' couple but is often found wanting when it comes to the prevention of physical bonding. Thus, monogamy in all its virtue reduces potentially spiritually and emotionally fulfilling experiences between two people to 'affairs' or in many cases sex and sex only. In turn guilt could be seen to help legitimise the notion of sex purely for pleasure and the culture of just using people as a means to personal gain as opposed to mutual gain. The fact that we go from one relationship to another tells us the idea of the perfect person or

Mr and Mrs "Right" is obviously flawed. We often like our new partners in different ways to old ones, basically because they placate different facets of our personality. They free us up to explore areas of ourselves hitherto closed by the perimeters of our last, or for that matter, our present relationship. The 'right' person is nothing more than a collection of others in exactly the same way that our social experience is fulfilled by an extensive range of friendships and acquaintances. In short, one person cannot supply what you need. You do not marry a supermarket; you marry a corner shop. It does not matter how late it stays open you cannot buy everything you need. In any case, even if it is possible for one person to satisfy our emotional and physical needs in totality, realistically, what is the chance of finding him or her? I hazard a guess that the chance of coming across our emotional mirror is virtually nil let alone doing just that and finding them attractive. This highlights another fault of founding relationships on monogamy.

The 'looks' factor is another area of relationships shrouded in the myths of "wouldn't it be nice if this was true". Men, on the whole, marry the best looking woman they can find, initially at any rate. With experience, men may see that trying to change someone beautiful but dull into someone beautiful and interesting is, in fact, an effort not worth the gamble. Women are better at this game from the outset. However, I am not saying that looks are not important to women, merely more easily overlooked where matters of money, status and security are concerned. Ask yourself when you last saw a woman on the arm of an aesthetically incompatible gentleman who was poor.

I am playing with clichés but, nevertheless, it is very

debatable as to the negative role monogamy plays when choosing partners for life. Despite the inevitability of the ageing process, the extent to which the monogamous premise blinds people to making good all round informed decisions is probably misjudged. Simply, do we marry for many reasons or do we marry 'looks' for many reasons. Certainly where the young are concerned the latter is dominant. In younger relationships and many older, possibly less experienced relationships marrying a body over its contents is, indeed, common. This is so as a direct consequence of the notion of being faithful. However, this is like marrying a wonderful food shop that never replenishes its stock. At first we glut ourselves, then for a while we will eat what they have not managed to sell, but it is not long before things are stale and not long after that, inedible.

So, marrying for the wrong reasons is generally fine until the so-called "spark" wears off. Then the fun begins. It is time to desperately try to persuade oneself how much this person really is the right one for you and this is normally done by trying to persuade one's friends. The sad outcome of this, for some of us, is that when we are with our loved ones we are never natural enough to enjoy it because we are in a constant mental dialogue of doubt, a conversation with oneself, born of monogamy.

Two main points arise then: no one person can provide all you need and against an environment of proliferated choice that realisation is far more apparent to us, with the obvious negative implications for the system of monogamy plain for all who care to look. It is worth noting here that the term "all you need" is not being used in a purely sexual way.

Unreal choice

Intrinsic to the concept of choice is of course comparison, in itself a useful tool in the process of decision-making. However, comparing reality with reality is one thing but comparing reality with fake reality is another. Modern life bombards us with fake reality. Films, media hype, adverts, the plastic surgeon and computer enhancement have effectively perverted our instinct to compare the lover we have with the lover we do not have and, inevitably, our sense of discomfort is heightened damaging our confidence in the partner we have. I challenge anyone questioning their relationship to see a "feel good" movie jam-packed with "beautiful" people in fantastic locations leading an exciting life, not to come out feeling bad. Obviously, we are aware of a superficiality/reality distinction and the fact that life is not like that but, nonetheless, it is a genuinely new phenomenon and does little to endorse contentment.

The emancipation of women

The emancipation of women is the real key to problems of longevity in the modern relationship. The developments mentioned above have cultivated a more fertile environment for infidelity "for the masses" to flourish. Our basic natural desires and our ability to contain them, have to cope with far more choice for far longer. However, women gaining the freedom and rights previously denied to them have made it easier to react negatively to an environment of increasing unfaithfulness. An accurate assessment of the perceived increase in casual relationships is probably not possible. I think it quite safe to say that, compliance with "the one partner for life" ethos, has never been the case in a fair percentage of marriages from all backgrounds. If anything only a culture of containment existed. There is, however, little question over the consequences for long-standing relationships that women's liberation from the ownership of man has brought. In her book, *Anatomy of Love*, Fisher sums up the consequence in a nutshell. Newfound social and economic circumstances have produced two fundamental changes. General economic equality means not only can women leave an unfaithful husband or contemplate leaving her spouse to pursue her own desires, but, the caring male (no irony intended), finds it easier to leave a woman because social stigma has evaporated and, financially, she can look after herself. Obviously the provision of welfare would also have to be included in any economic explanation of growing infidelity and separation.

Conclusion to circumstantial change

As, presently, organised in pursuing monogamy we are simply agreeing to do something we cannot do, not over a long period of time at any rate. The sacrifice necessary to deliver such a promise is contradicting our sense of Reason. Verbally agreeing to do something only serves to exacerbate the problem in that we create the expectation of compliance. For example, if someone agrees to meet you at the cinema at seven and you end up standing in the cold for half an hour before seeing the film solo, you get annoyed and disgruntled. However, if they say they will try to come but might not be able to make it, when they fail to arrive you are disappointed but not angry. There is something extremely annoying when people promise to do things and then fail to deliver. If we accept that social changes have indeed undermined our ability to achieve the one sexual partner for life doctrine, then in order to achieve the objective of one partner for life, we need to re-articulate what it is we agree to do. A concrete example of re-articulation in response to circumstantial change can easily be found in marriage. The notion, a women should obey the head of the household in the era of equality, is quite simply preposterous. The implications for the stability of marriage if men seriously expected women to obey them would be disastrous, but this is exactly the kind of outmoded thinking that monogamy insists upon. Marriage vows have been adapted as far as obedience to husbands is concerned so when it comes to abandoning agreeing to do what cannot be done happily, we have the pedigree. But, have we the guts?

Conclusion

I said above that I believed at present we were in a paradigm of romantic idealism, (albeit an illusion of selfish 'romantic' pragmatism). However, the problem with paradigms, as Thomas Kuhn pointed out in his book *The Structure of Scientific Revolutions*, is that they become inflexible as they always have fixed assumptions. Thus scientists offering theories premised beyond the confines of paradigms are given only the time it takes to dismiss them, resulting in potentially profitable areas of research being overlooked. Kuhn was, of course, talking on the subject of scientific inquiry but the principle behind his criticism is very relevant to our discussion. If we see romantic marriage as a paradigm, as opposed to a previous era or paradigm, when women and their belongings were considered the property of man, then we can see that one whole outlook and practical application has been replaced with another. Indeed, when J. S. Mill first put pen to paper on the subject of equality for women he was well aware of the sort of problem Kuhn brought to our attention. Simply, equality of the sexes or equality of the rights of the sexes did not arise from the, hitherto, accepted premise that the female was basically inferior. After all, it said it in the Bible God made Man and then made women for men. In his 'The Subjection of Women' Mill writes:

> 'In every respect the burden is hard on those who attack an almost universal opinion. They must be very fortunate as well as unusually capable if they obtain a hearing at all. They have more difficulty in obtaining a trial, than any other litigants have in getting a verdict.'

With the emergence of equality the female vow of obedience has not only become obsolete, it is seen as an embarrassing anachronism of a past and thankfully bygone era. It appears to me that once again, given the conditions within which a modern marriage must try to survive, it is time for a fundamental re-think. With this re-think precipitating a, no doubt, long and turbulent voyage to the end of monogamy as a virtue and hence an objective. It is debatable whether there always has been a happiness deficiency endemic to the monogamous relationship. However, the modern marriage differs from its traditional counterpart in its failure to last. The continued central role of fidelity and its obsession with sex effectively spells the beginning of the end of the 'until death us do part' aspect of marriage. If ahead of us lies a society without family we face an unknown, arguably the final atomization of the human. Surely the time has come for rational western man to try to wrestle the beauty of love from the entrails of past superstition and protect itself from the onset of the phenomenon of serial monogamy, which does nothing more than mirror the throw away nature of contemporary consumerism. Throwing away a perfectly good partner for the latest fashion that has caught our eye.

Generally speaking, most people do actually act in accordance with sacrifice, moderation or self-control, but this sense of proportion is due to the dictates of Reason. However, there is no sense of proportion where sex in regard to monogamous relationships is concerned. I believe fidelity in line with other actions and emotions should be subject to the principle of Aristotle's 'virtuous mean' or in the sense I am adopting it, 'moderation theory'. Remember we are talking ultimately about happiness, and doing things to excess constantly is boring and so not in line with the good or ultimate happiness. Getting pissed with friends is great. It is living. Getting pissed every day is escaping.

Stopping well short of judging, this is where I make the distinction between a 'swingers' mentality and what I am arguing in favour of. I believe partner swapping and swinger's parties not to be wrong, just not the solution. This is due, as I see it, to the romance deficiency, its susceptibility to the "if it's too easy it's less rewarding" phenomenon and thus with time it gets boring. Also, although possibly to a lesser extent, it is culturally "too much too soon" for many who try. It is not easy for a culture to drop its values overnight. Thinking modern and feeling modern do not always go hand in hand. Thus I would argue 'swinging' can only find a context within a confined relationship but it will not replace the need for other relationships. It is erroneous to assume the unfaithful are purely sexually motivated.

Therefore, what I am arguing is our self-control in these matters find their appropriate arbiter. To wit, subject the notion of fidelity to the prudence of Reason and away from the dogma of religious doctrine and/or the dictates of negative pragmatism which has been masquerading as idealism (I shall hopefully clarify the ins and outs of what I call negative pragmatism in the next chapter). The main idea important at this juncture is that fidelity should lose its superiority complex and accordingly be brought into line with the likes of, aggression, respect, generosity and so on, where most of us do utilize our powers of Reason to moderate our behavior. And those who do not are not regarded as defenders of some superior morality but socially deficient. At present we agree to do something that I believe contradicts our drive for inner contentment because monogamy, in the context of the 'golden mean', has no virtue as it places behavior at the deficient end of the scale. This, remember, Aristotle saw as injurious to the individual. His argument is pretty straight forward in that too much or too little is inferior to just the right amount. If I have so much respect for others that I have little or no self-respect, there is no virtue and happiness remains allusive. Let's be honest, those with no self-respect are generally depressed to one degree or another. Self-deprecation buttressed with a good helping of self-respect, on the other hand, can be very becoming and in being so has found its 'mean'.

Of course the main problem with endorsing infidelity is that it has already suffered the indignity of being demonised and, is therefore, considered a vice. Obviously, as a vice it is intrinsically bad in itself and therefore ineligible for 'moderation theory' along with murder, greed, envy and all else malicious. Indeed, Aristotle himself blacklists infidelity from his theoretical line of virtue. However, it is certainly worth noting that Aristotle's views on marriage were not subjected to the sort of scrutiny normally associated with the man whose other enquiries have, arguably (along with Plato), had more influence on western thought than any other thinker. If you are a man the best age to get married is thirty-seven, and if you are a woman, the best age is seventeen. I will leave it to your imagination as to how old Aristotle and his second wife were when they wed. In fact when reading the biographical introductions to the great philosophers, having dashing goods looks and a natural way with women seems to have eluded the majority of them. So, it appears to me, the school of thought emphatic and unquestioning in its support for monogamy should be treated with due care. Perhaps here it is less of a case of "those who can do and those who can't teach" and more of a case of "those who can do and those who can't, deceive".

That said, a cheap aside does not in any meaningful way dismiss Aristotle's claim, nor for that matter the problem that monogamy is seen to be 'right' by the vast majority of us regardless of whether we practice it or not. However, the point remains that if Reason can no longer support the practice of monogamy, then its foundation cannot be justified in any appeal to the rationality which modernity has founded its values on (in the sense that the sphere of morality since the enlightenment has been free from the constraints of an all encompassing myth or religion). Therefore, justification for monogamy and its continued application can only be found in the realms of irrationality, or put another way, belief. Belief requires faith and faith implies confidence in the 'supernatural' or, as Immanual Kant would term the 'unknowable'. Once a practice has no rational basis, if its continued adherence brings with it disagreeable consequences, it is simply not good enough just to say "it is morally correct". Why is it correct and where does it get its authority from? I am not particularly endorsing a utilitarian perspective (morality driven by its consequences) I am merely arguing that for monogamy to imply evil there has to be some recourse to eternal truth, due to it being in direct contradiction to the dictates of Reason. Therefore, the question that must be asked of monogamy is this: in order to retain its status as a "non-negotiable ought", can monogamy justify itself as an atemporal transcendental eternal truth? Or to lose the jargon, in order to keep its fundamental claim to being the 'right' thing to do, is monogamy a truth for all people for all times because some decision-maker or some supreme knowledge outside of the world says so? If it cannot do so outside of its ever-deteriorating historical packaging, then monogamy as a notion must subject itself to Reason.

Another objection that of course needs to be addressed is that Reason is being used to discuss a topic, which frankly is "none of its business". Remember my initial assumption based on the Aristotelian model is that most people would want their ideal relationship to be happy, life-long and as an individual's action, be founded in the 'Good'. Surely here the 'Good' should be interpreted as 'Love' and 'Love' is not the servant of Reason. Relationships and marriage are the stuff of love, aren't they? So to rationalise away something so pure is a mistake. Love is the essence of a marriage, and it is from this, not the rather austere credentials of Reason, that trust and respect develop for one's partner. Therefore, monogamy is a natural human response to basically being in love with someone.

It appears then that out of the discussion so far, two fundamental questions need to be answered. The first being; does monogamy have its origins in an absolute truth? And if so, is it not therefore ultimately a question of morality and not Reason? Secondly, is not monogamy a manifestation of love, and therefore not actually a question of Reason at all?

Chapter Two

Love, Virtue and Monogamy

'The dishonour that accompanies a lie also accompanies the liar like his shadow.'

(Immanuel Kant)

'Cynicism is the closest common souls come to honesty.'

(Friedrich Nietzsche)

In all the discussions and debates I have had on the subject of monogamy, three main ideas always surface, albeit to varying degrees. Firstly, there is the idea that love and monogamy are inseparable, secondly, infidelity and immorality (or at least *wrong-doing*) are also inseparable and thirdly, to a lesser extent, monogamy is *natural* to man due to our predisposition to pair for the purpose of family. I have no problem with these ideas being discussed, only with the non-negotiable manner or 'given' nature with which people introduce them into the conversation. Of course, there are a great many of us who would disagree with the above. However, those who do, have probably, believed in the first two if not all three at some point in their lives. But in a sense this is exactly my point. We have had to discover it all for ourselves because very few parents tell children anything to the contrary.

Implicit in the monogamist defence and, indeed, the manner with which they defend their position, is that the two questions that came out of the discussion in the previous chapter are simply never asked. Thus, where fidelity is concerned, there exists in our culture today, a perception of failure. In addition, criticism is confined only to those actions that perpetuate any such perceived failure. Hence, comments such as "acting stupidly", "selfishly" or "symptomatically", for example, are criticisms of actions without any criticism of the fundamental tenant of monogamy as a goal. This continues to be the case despite the context of spiraling divorce rates and 27% citing infidelity as the reason. Moreover, just because the other two thirds or so do not actually separate for that reason it does not preclude the possibility that adultery has occurred within any such relationship. In any case what we are dealing with here is an assumption with an extremely high failure rate. In fact, I would argue, it is now so flawed as to be untenable. Put it this way, if any assumption had such a high failure rate in any other prescriptive field, serious questions would be being asked. Indeed, within the medical profession those persons deemed to be responsible might well find themselves in court facing a charge of negligence. In addition, given greater medical recognition of mental problems being on a par with physical ones, and, given how much disturbance family breakdowns cause, surely we should be at least looking at the possibility that the presumptions of monogamy are not all they profess to be. After all being committed to a belief does not render us immune from having to answer appropriate questions of it. However, in order to genuinely re-examine our commitment to monogamy, both the questions raised at the end of chapter one, and the natural argument, require an answer but any such attempt should be done so, honestly. If they are not addressed it perhaps tells one more about a 'believer' than the belief. The third line of defence mentioned above – that humans have a 'natural' admiration for fidelity with the purpose of family in mind – will hopefully be addressed within the following discussion of the first two questions.

Love and Monogamy

Broadly speaking, most people, when confronted with someone saying that they are not prepared to be monogamous, instinctively question the point of that person bothering to enter into a 'serious' relationship in the first place. Implicit in the "what's the point in getting married" response, is that being faithful is the "be all and end all" when it comes to being involved in a 'serious' relationship. This sentiment is often expressed as "if you *really* love someone you do not want to be unfaithful". Thus we have this notion that monogamy is the product of love.

Let us for a moment take the hypothesis that if you *really* love someone, you do not want to sleep with anybody else. Is this true? No doubt, for many it is. In my independent survey, 89% of those asked if they believed the above statement to be true, said that they did. However, the logical conclusion of this statement dictates that when one is unfaithful, one must by definition, no longer be in love with one's partner. Yet, when this second statement was put to my straw poll (minus mitigation: alcohol / drugs etc) only 31% of those asked said that they believed this to be true. Therefore, two-thirds of those poled do not actually believe what they think they believe. It is also worth noting that the vast majority of the 31% whose view was consistent, took much longer to answer the second statement than they did to the first.

Another objection to the "if you really love someone you wouldn't sleep with someone else" assumption is that under closer inspection it holds more than just an actual 'fact' and is in fact making two further claims. Firstly, monogamy has a monopoly where 'real' love is concerned. Secondly, it also maintains, that 'true' or 'real' love is indeed definable and the monogamous fraternity openly accept love to be conditional. In that if you break our trust, my love, in any meaningful practical sense, will die. To wit, I will not want to be with you anymore. Therefore, love is conditional on not sleeping with anybody else, even if, as under some interpretations of the rule of monogamy, you are permitted to want to – the "you are allowed to look, but you cannot touch" mentality. Encapsulated then, in the unwavering "we're right and if you don't agree you're wrong" quasi-religious method of argument is basically the following sentiment: we know what love is. It *can* be defined. It *is* conditional and we are right because it is true; even though two-thirds of us don't actually believe ourselves.

The necessary relationship between love and fidelity has fragile logic and therefore must be in some doubt. Charles Pierce, writing in the 19th century, identified four methods of settling doubt, which he considered the basic purpose of all inquiry. The first approach was one of tenacity. This involves choosing any answer and maintaining it by taking any actions necessary. This of course also requires everybody to think the same way. This is one interpretation of how western societies have approached the question of monogamy. We have simply chosen as a culture to embrace it and to a great extent over come the method of tenacity's main drawback that of wholesale conformity. Obviously, the problem being that any such conformity is limited to the theoretical sphere. So we are prepared to use the pejorative language associated with infidelity such as 'cheating' and 'sordid affairs' etc without the necessary actions to back up our belief in it. Hence, with a growing division between words and action, bordering on the hypocritical, settled belief will naturally be disturbed with fresh doubt.

The second method of removing doubt, Pierce noted, involves the masses bowing to the decrees of some authoritative body. Again here, we can see this method as having been applied through the Christian religion's laws permeating through western societies. Once, however, religious belief wanes inevitably the authoritarian method of settling this particular inquiry is inadequate and then relies on the first method for its continuation.

The third method was that of Reason, the benefit of which being that it secured free will and independent decisions. This, according to Pierce, was preferable to the former two but left belief at the mercy of fashion and, hence, truth contingent. Pierce was talking of the philosophical Reason this being theoretical and in no need of experience as such. Rationalist philosophical schools were skeptical of objects and the real world and forwarded that truth could be arrived at through purely intellectual paths.

For a 'father of pragmatism' questioning the reality of what the senses offered was of little practical use. Therefore, for Pierce, only the scientific method with its belief in reality independent of opinion could be the true arbiter to what *really* was and *was* not. The role of Reason was thus limited to interpreting experience into 'laws'. Effectively this approach could be summed up in the words of realist John Alston when he states:

'a proposition or belief is only true if, and only if, what the statement says to be the case actually is the case'.

And in addition a proposition, within the fallibilist approach, is true and only true until it is proven not to be the case. This is most commonly illuminated in the example "all swans are white until you see a black one". How one finds whether something is the case or not is, of course, achieved basically by testing the proposition with actual experience. The scientific method starts with a proposition or glorified guess. It then calculates the consequences of any such hypothesis and then tests experience to see if those consequences do in fact exist. If they do not, no matter how nice an idea it is, the hypothesis is wrong.

When looking for the 'Truth' we have to at least recognise there are two schools of thought. Truth is either objective or subjective. The objective camp believe in absolutist principles of universal truths and range from philosophers with their great meta-narratives (big stories) of how things all hang together, to the world religions and of course the scientists. All agree that truth lies outside of the individual but that is about all they agree on. The subjective camp, another broad church of ideas, believes truth comes from within or is made up by ourselves and is therefore at best (socially speaking) what is generally agreed and at worst (socially speaking) what anybody decides is true for themselves.

The verification model is the only one that will satisfactorily lead to an objective answer as to the relationship between love and monogamy. Obviously it is debatable as to whether this is a suitable method of inquiry where the nature of emotions are in question. Nonetheless, it is very useful because outside of this method any truth in the matter can only be subjective. In other words it is up to the individual, which by definition leaves the assertion of a necessary relationship between love and monogamy derelict. So, whilst there is in fact a lot to be said for an existential approach, the problem with leaving truth to subjectivity is that it leaves this question wide open to the problems of the first three methods of inquiry outlined above. In other words, if truth is going to be inventing and not discovering, then to avoid the perils of the tenacious and authoritative methods of settling doubt, we all have to be 'inventors' and not passively rely on the discoveries of 'other inventors'. Indeed, the point of looking for an answer in objective truth in this particular matter is that it at least provides the individual an opportunity to escape the imperialism of 'hand me down' moral and romantic opinion. And in doing so offers space for genuine individual reflection and hence more authentic opinion. If truth or a 'more important' truth lies in the subjectivity of individual human existence and not simple objective truths, let's make it *genuinely* subjective.

So, our hypothesis then is this: monogamy is the product of real love, or at least the desire of real love. If we then calculate the consequence of our proposition, we should find the world or at least, the west, full of successful, happy relationships where adultery is confined to an extreme minority of couples and divorce being kept to a minimum and confined generally to non-sexual matters of dispute. However, when we look out into the real world to see if our prediction tallies with everyday life, what we find is far from the idyllic consequences we expected.

Simply, people are not particularly happy. Infidelity, or at least the desire of it, is rife and detected unfaithfulness is the most cited reason of 'documented' divorce. If you think this to be a very presumptuous and generalised statement, then fine, may be it is. However, this is where individual honesty must play its crucial role if ever we are to accept an answer as truth and, to use William Barrett's phrase, 'what is more severe than honesty'.

It appears to me then, that due to the failure of our hypothesis to meet the requirements of the Verification Principle, only two conclusions can be drawn. One is that simply the guess is wrong. Love is, in fact, not linked to monogamy, certainly in any absolutist sense. Or two, the hypothesis is right. However, if the hypothesis is correct it indicates that real love cannot last for life for the vast majority of us. Indeed, if we go along with the anthropologists, true love has a life span of about four years. This is because if the proposition is true, by definition, when we are unfaithful we must have fallen out of love. Naturally then, in the context of preserving the longevity of marriage and the protection of family life, true love paradoxically becomes no basis for long term commitment as it can only last for a relatively short time. My personal view is that the second conclusion is complete nonsense and only has legitimacy in the notion of romance and the passion of the "Just met" scenario and has nothing to do with *real* love.

So, if monogamy is not an expression of love, what is it an expression of? In the first chapter I introduced the notion of what I call 'negative pragmatism' and it is this, which is where I believe the key to the love and monogamy proposition lies.

Love or negative pragmatism?

When people put forward the idea that fidelity is an expression of love or the natural bonding of two lovers, it all sounds beautiful, and is on the surface a seemingly powerful natural argument. Initially, this 'indisputable' defence of monogamy then has all the strength and beauty of polished virtue. However, the more monogamists are pushed to defend their position, it gets rather circular and has a certain "it is right because it is right" ring to it. Continued exposure to assumptions hitherto never really confronted, their argument starts to show its rather less grandiose, functional foundations. It is not long before monogamy is being defended with questions of a very practical nature. What if they are better in bed than you? Or, what if a new lover is more attractive? What if this or that is bigger than this or that? In other words, what if they like the other person more than one? Or more to the point, and crucially, what if my partner leaves me? All of a sudden it sounds like monogamy has lost its intrinsic relationship with love, and is merely a vehicle to protect oneself against personal loss. I am not for one minute trying to trivialise what is no doubt an extremely sensitive area. Indeed to the contrary, the fear of loss is something very much to be reckoned with. However, insecurity should be seen for what it is and should not be allowed to clothe itself in the platitudes of deep love. The proposition that monogamy is a good idea because it reduces the chances of couples leaving each other is something very different from the proposition that monogamy is the ambassador of real love. In its very practicality, can be seen a pragmatic response to a negative set of emotions and effectively monogamy is western culture's surrender to insecurity.

That said, the practical objection in general, is one that cannot be ignored. However, this assumption is inherent in the assumption that monogamy is the way things *should* be. And, as I outlined in the first chapter, the idea that monogamy actually keeps people together in the present circumstances is frankly very suspect. It may have a delaying quality. However a common scenario, often unnoticed, is that when people fancy someone else if they have faith in monogamy they are more likely to separate in order to have the person they want and keep their principle intact. In addition, if monogamy is agreed at the outset of a relationship it is more likely to cause irrevocable damage to such a relationship. In short, far from acting as an agent of cohesion, when honesty prevails, it is more likely to drive a wedge between people. Another, yet interrelated, response to the practical objection is this; letting your partner 'experience others', at present involves sexual pleasure but still denies romantic bonding. You can 'fuck' them but you cannot 'make love' to them. However, if what is desired is the retrieval of romance and *not* just fulfilling the demands of lust, then people experiencing affairs will want to leave their partner precisely to free themselves to bond emotionally with their new lover. Only by separating can they achieve what is desired in the first place. And without contradiction, merely addition, a third less speculative response is simply that for most people the actual act does not mean a lot. Very few people will actually leave the security for the sex anyway. Indeed, I suggest many of the unfaithful fraternity have experienced great sex with a great body but not felt the urge to leave someone they love and care deeply for. If this is so, why is it they cannot afford the same capacity to their partner, who after all is supposed to be in love with them? The answer to this is of course jealousy; the very lungs of monogamy breathing in all that is good, and exhaling the foul breath of all that is bad. Monogamy is the slave of jealousy not the servant of love. Monogamy is the cancer of love, making it conditional, seeking to confine it, mould it and shape it. Love cannot be carved; it can only be felt and to make love conditional is to make it something else.

Nonetheless, when defending monogamy from the premise of love, ironically, jealousy is brought in as a "big gun" of its offensive repartee. The line of argument is normally that there is some sort of intuitive tendency to admire fidelity, thus the desire to be monogamous is natural for the sake of family; and it is from this well that our jealousy springs. In other words, our jealousy is a kind of natural adhesive for family life. Therefore, the emotion of jealousy at its most raw atavistic level is being used to justify the practice of monogamy. So, once again, the real love notion starts to lose its gloss, as the practice of monogamy now is apparently some sort of inbred pragmatic response to the nature of Man.

This line of argument does not, however, tie in with the traditional and compelling anthropological explanation of why infidelity is in actual fact so frequent an occurrence. Very briefly the argument is as follows: men find as many partners as possible in order to ensure their genes are reproduced; and women naturally look for a multiple of partners to try to ensure they are impregnated with best quality sperm. So, if we accept both positions then we are left with a natural tendency to be jealous of others doing what, as an animal, we are naturally programmed to do. Once again, albeit not necessarily of biblical proportions, it seems mankind is doomed to the fate of eternal contradiction, in that our disposition is one of instinctually wanting to sleep around but not wanting our partners to. Of course these positions effectively concede that man is in fact just another species. However, if we believe that language, an innate self awareness and the power of Reason do indeed free ourselves from the inevitability of natural design, then as humans we should be capable of determining our own behavior and in turn see sexual jealousy as conquerable.

However, my fundamental point is this. When pushed, the 'real' love defenders of monogamy, once their fragile shell of 'respect' and 'trust' is penetrated, ultimately rest their argument on responding to the problems of jealousy on one hand, and fear of losing their partner, on the other. Both, most would agree, are negative elements within our personalities; after all a great deal of psychotherapy is dedicated to helping people face, and hopefully overcome their insecurities. Accusations of jealousy, outside of the sexual sphere, are something we instinctively deny. If we are embarrassed by our jealousy we must see it as something undesirable. So, in my view, they are both undesirable. They also have a causal relationship with monogamy. Therefore, the idealism of monogamy is a myth. What is ideal in placating these undoubted emotional bullies? I think, "respect my insecurity" and "trust my jealousy", in the end, is a more honest reflection of the 'real' love idealist sentiment. Only when we accept this, can we free ourselves from the Kantian shadow of dishonor.

Most therapists would agree that half the battle of an alcoholic is to accept that he or she is one. Admitting to oneself that we indeed do have a problem opens the door to potential solutions. I believe recognising the practice of monogamy to be endorsing a policy of negative pragmatism is imperative if we are to have any chance of ending the perpetual paradox of relationships. Nonetheless, admitting one's problems does not by itself solve them, which leaves the very real and problematic question of dealing with jealousy and the fear of loss and its implicit loneliness. Without professing to have any 'wave of the wand answers' I will offer the following suggestions.

In the case of jealousy, like most other questions of human development, there is always the nature/nurture consideration. I have never been very convinced by the strict Empiricist position, which holds that *everything* is 'learned' through social reinforcement. However, if here I am mistaken then the simple (if somewhat flippant) answer to our problem is to reinforce differently in order to eradicate jealousy. That said, if jealousy is not wholly the product of such reinforcement and has a substantial instinctive element, simply reinforcing different values would not, in itself, help our striving towards happiness. This is because we would have a situation where there would be a multiplicity of jealous responses to perfectly socially acceptable sexual behaviour. Such a situation would hardly be conducive to our goal of happiness and long lasting couples. Just as a multiplicity of jealous responses to unacceptable social behaviour does not which happens at present.

Let us then, for the sake of argument, accept that there is an unlearned, innate sexual jealousy inherent in the human condition. Given such a scenario, I believe the key to progress is still to embark on a project of reinforcing values, but doing so in full recognition of, and without being complacent about, the disruptive force of instinctive jealousy. If we accept that jealousy is natural, the question we have to answer is does that make monogamy a necessarily correct response? After all, is not aggression a natural instinct? Being the "hardest", however, no longer in rational, civilised society qualifies one for power. Nor for that matter is settling differences through violence, the first course of action for the majority of us. In short, we fetter naturally anti social tendencies in our children. Another example is selfishness. When a child is being selfish we do not take a course of action that rewards that selfishness. We teach the child through various mechanisms to be ashamed of itself and in doing so, fetter what is nothing less than natural behaviour. Indeed, as mentioned above jealousy in other areas of life is something we are "conditioned" to be self-regulating in. We basically get jealous, but any recrimination for the situation is generally directed at our selves for feeling so. The accusation "you're just jealous" is almost always met with a denial. In all these areas our emotions are 'moulded' before being allowed to enter the fray of adult life.

Where matters of the heart are concerned on the other hand, no such fettering occurs. In fact, as a society, we positively encourage this pure negative emotion. "You're right to feel like this". "It's only natural, well done". This approach brings love down to the sewers of untreated human jealousy. Therefore, as we have through Reason learned to control our more atavistic tendencies in the pursuit of a greater more valuable living experience, I suggest we remove the privilege of immunity that sexual jealousy enjoys and make it available to education and fettering from childhood onwards. Then, when confronted with inevitable pangs of jealousy we will tend to self-regulate in these matters as we do in all other areas of natural inclination. With this at the heart of an altogether more honest approach to the nurturing of expectations, perhaps future generations will be better equipped to step beyond the paralysis of the tension between natural fear and jealousy and the natural disposition for unilateral infidelity. It is important to remember that this claim is not suggesting that everybody wants to go around sleeping with everybody else all the time. I am merely saying that eventually many people do, and in the future the "eventually", under the pressure from the increasing irrationality of monogamy, will be sooner rather than later.

The general associational reinforcement referred to above, I think, will help to address the question of how we go about treating insecurity. However, this is the underlying subject matter of chapters three and four and so for now, best left until later. At this stage, it is only necessary to recognise its negativity and moreover the causal relationship between insecurity and monogamy.

Conclusion to Love and Monogamy

At the end of chapter one, the second objection to monogamy being subjected to the theoretical virtuous mean as I have adapted it, was the proposition that Reason had no primary role to play where marriage is concerned. Its role was a subservient one involving no more than the organisation of practical day to day ramifications, of *being in love*. The question then posed was; is the assumption that monogamy is the expression of true love and respect correct? In this chapter, I have argued that this assumption is flawed and that being faithful is not a consequence of being in love, unless being in love is enforcing our partners to submit to the dictates of personal insecurities and jealousy. Whether one wraps this in the language of respect and trust and so on and so forth or not, it is inherently selfish. The only love I see is self-love. And under such circumstances monogamy is at best a mutual agreement for two people to love themselves but not each other.

Virtue and Monogamy

It appears to me that authority for monogamy must lie outside the province of love. In turn our allegiance to monogamy, in order to be justified, is forced to posit its authority in the realms of virtue. This then brings us to the other question posed at the end of chapter one. Namely, is monogamy of virtue in itself? In using the term virtue, I mean one of two criteria. Either the practice of monogamy has intrinsic moral worth over and above accountability to any consequence. Or, the practice of monogamy has virtue through the mechanism of cultural consent grounded, not in the irrational, but in common sense. The difference between the two is the source from which the value is derived from.

Under the first criteria, that of intrinsic moral worth, the source is one of faith, in that its authority lies *outside* the jurisdiction of facts and ultimately lies in the notion of eternal truth. The idea being; there exists a timeless set of universal ideals with which to measure behaviour against. Whilst there have been philosophers who professed these 'truths' to be available to the intellect, the ultimate source of authority for eternal truth essentially lies in some form of Godhead. There is obviously a problem of putting forward a proposition that something is right because "God says so". Whether it is a conclusion reached via rigorous academic pursuit or blind unquestioning belief, it cannot be proved one way or the other. Therefore, when all is said and done, virtue when posited in the demands of eternal truth is inspired by faith. The trouble with faith, of course, is one of relativity in that we find our own reassuring, but can often find other people's rather disturbing. And if Kierkegaard is right in identifying faith as an individual's 'leap' beyond Reason, then arbitration between conflicting faiths is frankly hopeless and a waste of time.

The second criteria, I would argue, is essentially 'ends' orientated. By which I mean the 'goal' or 'end' dictates the agenda when deciding what a virtue *is*, or what is valued and what is not. So, in this sense, virtue is a post fact experience designed to eliminate behavior at odds with some designated goal. To put it another way, our values are reactive and have been shaped by reality.

For example, let us take the case of "Thou shall not kill". Is murder bad because it is evil? Or is it evil (and therefore bad) because of the consequences of such action? (The consequences being for society, the general lawlessness that endless retribution would induce). If it is the former then 'not killing' as a value is founded in some intuitive, arguably innate sense of right and wrong. People, in which case, do not refrain from murdering out of respect to some unwritten contractual obligation to the state, nor do they refrain from murdering out of fear of life imprisonment or whatever punishment may be meted out to them. The action is seen as having value in itself. Therefore, the action has its inspiration in 'faith', in that murder is reviled in the context of a *belief* attached to the umbilical chord of eternal truth which denounces the killing of innocents as wrong. However, there is a perfectly rational explanation, propounded, as well as anyone, by Thomas

Hobbes in his *Leviathan*. Hobbes tells us that without the State life would be 'nasty brutish and short'. Therefore, the 'innate' belief that murder is wrong would be absent in many and so, with the goal of self preservation in mind, we forfeit our natural right to violence in return for the protection of our freedom and property. In this way, the state has a monopoly of violence to enforce a law founded on an agreed principle. Thus, society holds the preservation of life as a value without necessary recourse to supernatural external law. The virtue then lies very much within the human sphere as it is inspired by our powers of Reason.

My point is this. For the sake of argument, let us, for a moment, agree that the value of 'not killing' actually has its origins in the 'fact' of murder and its negative consequences. Under such circumstances, the virtue, has its inspiration fundamentally in Reason and not, *belief.* In that, it is a common sense law to prevent the predicted consequences, (albeit common sense perhaps also deemed it prudent not to undermine its supernatural status as a law of God). The crux of the matter then, is this; whether or not "Thou shall not kill" has its inspiration in the supernatural or social human pragmatism or both, it does not actually matter. This is so because they both bring about the desired response. The crucial point, however, is that they both do so because there is no conflict between 'Faith' and 'Reason'. Obviously, from both a philosophical and theological perspective, the source of our virtue does matter. But these somewhat abstract debates rarely breach the frontiers of specialised academia into the experience of the general populace. So, it only really matters for the average member of society, when there is a conflict between the prescriptions of Faith and Reason, and matters most, when that conflict is interfering in the practical day-to-day running of our lives. I suggest, in the case of monogamy, we do have a problem in that its virtue status as informed by Reason is in serious doubt. And so, there is a genuine, if largely unrecognised, conflict with our inherited sense of 'Faith' in monogamy as a virtue.

Put it this way, the truism "You don't regret the things that you did, only the things that you didn't", in the case of murder, does not apply. What sort of person regrets not killing someone? However, only the reader can honestly answer whether or not the old adage applies to their love life.

People do have affairs, lovers and desires, but generally they do not go around killing each other. Obviously, it could be just because it is a far lesser crime or 'sin'. However, my argument is that in this area, faith no longer has the parallel support of Reason because of the reasons discussed in chapter one. After all many of us would still feel an inherent sense of wrong merely by stealing a few pence worth of sweets from our local shop keeper. But once again, confronted with the acid test of action, how many of the 'unfaithful' would not steal or kill?

There does exist, in my opinion, a clash between the two potential sources of monogamy's value, albeit simmering just beneath conscious thought. And it is this clash which is derailing our ultimate inherent drive towards happiness. Yet the drive to happiness is not just lying down and "accepting its lot". It is motivating change at a level of action hitherto unprecedented. Unfortunately, however, people are changing partners in preference to changing their perception of monogamy as a virtue. Hence, the continued belief in the 'rightness' of monogamy in a rational environment which is hostile to it is producing divorce and separation and plunging us into the instability and transience of serial monogamy. What is worse, we are all patting ourselves on the back at having found the "future" of relationships.

Reason is our rudder in an ever-changing world, allowing us the freedom to adjust behavior to circumstance. However, it is also the tool with which we seek truth even if Reason eventually has to accept that 'truth' rests beyond its grasp. To go beyond Reason, however, requires belief. So if monogamy is to remain a 'pure' virtue, in the sense that it is not required to define its value in terms of just the right amount of application, (as do 'lesser' emotions such as courage and so on) then the tension between Reason and belief must be resolved. Any resolution, however, must find in favour of faith. Without such authority, the continued practice will represent nothing short of a stubborn refusal to accept the age and circumstance we live in. Think for a second of the fifty-something bloke trying to pull in a club or the sixty something woman dressing forty years her junior. Much in the same way, there is something very unsightly about a virtue, defined as a value from a fact, refusing to accept the age that it lives in.

Faith and monogamy

In a letter to his sister explaining why he was abandoning a career in theology, Friedrich Nietzsche wrote:

> 'Every true faith is infallible. It performs what the believing person hopes to find in it but it does not offer the least support for the establishing of an objective truth. Here the ways of men divide. If you want to achieve peace of mind and happiness have faith. If you want to be a disciple of truth, then, search.'

Adultery or infidelity must be a question of belief, and belief, though potentially still the product of deep intellectual investigation, in the end relies on placing truth outside of the world. It must be an *'ought'* to be the case, regardless of what Reason demands and therefore must have its authority in an external arbiter. That arbiter then has to be some kind of God. Although, fidelity was valued in pre-Christian Greek philosophy, it is in the Judeo-Christian tradition where monogamy is most revered. Truth is here posited in the rules and regulations set out by the Ten Commandments. Therefore, the role of Reason is subordinate to the demands of Faith. This cosmological outlook characterised the whole of medieval life where the lure of the 'next life' imprisoned the desires of emotion and natural impulses of Reason in the present life. Despite the fact that most factions of the practicing Christian fraternity teach the Christian message with different emphases in line with their own brand of biblical selectivity and interpretation, there is a basic conformity where sexual morality is concerned. It is, however, not the purpose of this essay to investigate theological disputes. The simple point is that when discussing the topic of sexual fidelity we need to divide monogamists into two camps: those who have faith and those who do not. The first group, being the practicing Christians whose obedience to monogamy is founded in religious law and the second and much larger monogamist community being those from a secular background. Paradoxically the average monogamist, it seems, is probably the most selective Christian of them all. This is because they are only Christians when it comes to relationships and the assumption of monogamy. The average monogamist does not actually believe in God as defined in the Christian tradition. They do not go to church, do not pray before meals and consider 'happy-clappy Jeremy' with his "Jesus is in my guitar" song, generally, a bit of a wally. Even the more reflective mature schools of Christian thought, are rarely afforded little more than an "each to their own" shrug by the average agnostic.

Paradoxically, the secular monogamist's 'faith' in monogamy has no faith to draw on and so, in turn, fails to provide the comfort of infallibility that Nietzsche speaks of. This is not to accept Nietzsche's cynicism wholesale, merely to recognise that the Christian who has faith believes in the infallibility of Religious law, and therefore is far less exposed to the tensions between Reason and feeling that dog his or her secular counterpart. Of course, this does not mean that the devout do not stray, but undoubtedly it is in the secular community where most infidelity occurs.

The problem then, for the secular monogamist, is one of grounding their practice, as a virtue, because virtue is either grounded in Faith or Reason. However, monogamy, I argue, can no longer be grounded in Reason given its failing prescriptive use for relationships, due to its inability to "deliver the goods" where matters of happiness and stability are concerned. It is also unacceptable to ground secular monogamy in some inner non-specified belief system because that ignores the underlying reason for wanting to do so. By which, I mean, the culture of Judeo-Christian traditions that has permeated those desires in the first place. For, if it is not the result of enculturative conditioning, (anthropological jargon for the values one is brought up with) and there is in fact, some sort of intuition of nature being latched onto, then why don't we practice it more? Furthermore, why isn't monogamy universal to all cultures and why haven't anthropologists located a monogamous human society ever? Not one that has not been subjected to the 'truths' of religious revelation at any rate. Without faith then, the secular community, are left with an argument which sounds suspiciously like "monogamy is right because it is right". Moreover, if there is no God in the religious sense i.e. a rule setting God, then the secular monogamist has the problem that monogamy as a practice is de-deified, so man must have made it up. It is also, more often than not the case that when man makes up rules they tend to be for a *reason*. But rules for a reason, based on Reason, tend to be at the mercy of circumstance. (A quick glance at an old football rulebook would demonstrate how rules have to change to accommodate the demands of changing circumstance and to maintain the ultimate aim of the sport, which is entertainment). Initially, the reason was that God demanded it, but if in seeking the truth we do not accept religious authority, but still continue to practice a tradition anchored in the supernatural, it is now because man, and not God, demands it. But if man now demands monogamy there can be no universal underpinning to monogamy's claim to virtue. Without this foundation the secular monogamist cannot ground the morality of monogamy in anything. They are confronted with a belief vacuum in that there is then no reason whatsoever to practice an action that they do. Hence, it is of little surprise that in reality they quite often do not. Yet it is an action held dear and of great importance, though, inherently damaging to their pursuit of happiness. The secular monogamist can therefore be charged with the very irrationality secularism seeks to avoid, and often disdains in the platitudes of evangelism. Hence secular monogamists are, perhaps, the greatest of all selective Christians.

There is, however, one philosopher who, arguably alone throws secular monogamy a foundational life line. In response to reading David Hume's empiricist philosophy that denounced any objective truth outside of experience, Immanuel Kant placed truth in *duty* not *happiness*. Morality was a question of obligation and available to all, through the faculties of practical reason. In the respect his system offers universality without 'knowledge of revelation'. Secular monogamy could find refuge in Kantian morality, which manifests itself in what he termed the Categorical Imperative. This maxim states: 'act only on the maxim you can will to be a universal law' or as Michael Macrone helpfully translates it 'do unto others as you would have everyone do unto everybody'. Basically, before acting, ask yourself the question, what if every body did that? Obviously, if everybody stayed faithful then arguably there would be far less of a problem in terms of separation. However, it is very difficult to square the self-discipline and deference to duty as opposed to happiness required to enact Kant's system, with the modern living tendencies of throw away capitalist culture, or for that matter, the overall aim of a person's life.

Nevertheless, according to Kant man's freedom is derived from his capacity to make moral decisions and is then the best chance for secular monogamy to ground itself, and therefore, have some weight when 'ideally' determining or guiding moral behaviour. In short, the Kantian ethic avoids relativism yet keeps absolutism bereft of traditional Christian metaphysics. So, the secular monogamist could invoke the message in Kant's adaptation of the Golden Rule of 'do unto others ...' and defend monogamy's claim to "pure virtue" in terms of; if every-body was faithful to everybody then marriages would survive.

However, this position is not unproblematic. Firstly, making a commitment to monogamy, as pointed out earlier, in no way guarantees the longevity of relation-ships. Separation may well occur in order to avoid infidelity and, thus, is more the tool of serial monogamy. Secondly, again mentioned above, it neglects the question of happiness. Inbuilt is the surrender of happiness, in the name of duty. And, thirdly, if one accepts my earlier argu-ment that monogamy, outside of the initial throws of romance, is in actual fact at root in deference to fear and jealousy, then we would appear to be advocating a policy of universalising negativity. It is difficult to square the universalising of jealousy and personal hang-ups with acting in accordance to a moral principle. Certainly, if one compares that with a policy of universalising uncondi-tional love as acting in accordance to moral principle. Indeed, as a buttress to a stable relationship, it neither competes virtuously nor practically. Unconditional love has a greater chance of hurdling the 'infidelity problem' because, essentially, it does not demand it, and is by nature more forgiving, if and when, our jealousies and insecurities are impinged upon. Furthermore, if we look at the second of Kant's ethical maxims he states that people should be treated as ends in themselves and therefore to use someone as a means to personal goals is to act uneth-ically. Here again, if we accept fear and jealousy are at the root of demanding our partners' faithfulness then their sacrifice is in violation of Kantian ethical principles. This is so because in the expectation of monogamy we *use* our spouses' fidelity as a coping mechanism. In as much that, our partners' actions become a 'means' to the end of our own security, in the face of our inability to cope with our jealousy and insecurity appropriately. Therefore, our partners are not in reality being treated as an 'end' in themselves sovereign over their individual actions. They are being treated as a means for selfish purposes. This is part of an overall tendency for long-term relationships to compromise inwardly. However, this "inward compromise" is a concept that I shall develop in chapter four.

Conclusion

What this boils down to is a question of purpose. What is the aim of monogamy? If the Judeo-Christian traditions are correct in their belief in monogamy as demanded by God then, as a virtue, it is what Thomas Auxter would call a 'passive' virtue. By this is meant that there is a 'pre-obligation to a higher value' and thus the purpose of monogamy is to satisfy omnipotent authority unquestioningly which results in 'the attempt to repress behaviour'. However, fidelity as a goal is not in isolation within religious faith and, therefore, there is less likelihood of being exposed to the negative consequences endured by the secular monogamist. Nonetheless, whether under God or just under the stars, 'active' virtue is about individual freedom through the power of Reason and is about 'creating a better world'. When the aim is to improve our living experience, obviously our virtues founded in Reason, in addition to experience, must always be done in the shadow of consequences. And since secular monogamy has no authenticity as a belief, it cannot be a 'passive' virtue. Moreover, being an 'active' virtue it is effectively admitting that it is not a "pure" virtue in the a priori sense. Therefore, to remain off the Aristotelian line of virtue or "moderation line" (which produces virtue, in that the application of an action or emotion, is done so in just the right quantity), it has to have the full support of Reason. In chapter one and in this chapter I have argued that monogamy with or without biblical authority is irrational and, given the ever changing circumstances, increasingly so. Therefore, there is a conflict between Reason and Faith where monogamy is concerned. In this chapter I have also argued that monogamy, to borrow Ingersol's phrase on prudery 'pretends to own the emotions it cannot feel' and as a consequence secular relationships are suspect to fragility, separation and unhappiness. This is not to say religious marriage is not immune to such consequences, but merely to a lesser degree.

I believe, therefore that both questions posed at the end of chapter one, have failed to provide a positive answer. Is monogamy endemic within the emotion of love? No. Is monogamy a virtue of eternal truth? No. There is, then, no good reason why fidelity should not find its virtue status through the appropriate mechanism of moderation and it is our present failure to do so *mentally* which needs to be addressed. I say mentally as presently our actions are, arguably, already in accordance with moderation theory. However, due to the disparity between what one does and individually feels, and what is collectively thought and expected as a culture, submission to Reason in action only is creating a bleak climate of serial monogamy.

Of course, it is highly questionable that we have ever wanted to be monogamous but, for arguments sake, let us accept it had greater support in yesteryear. Nonetheless, the idea of turning back the clock to keep families together in all its rhetoric of responsibility is in fact nothing short of highly irresponsible. Politicians and the moral fraternity are forever imploring us to return to perceived traditional family values. By itself this is simply silly or just cynical political expediency. We cannot return to past practices unless we can reset the circumstances within which they were enacted. For example, greater mobility through the motor car means we can meet more people and, thus, face more temptation because our indiscretions are more likely to go undetected. Patently, we are not going to return to the number of cars on the road in the 1930's or whatever. Perhaps it would be less effective, if that is possible, for writers of such speeches to say what they actually are saying; "please can everybody pretend to live in the past".

In order to restore parity to attitudes and actions, a more sensible route is to understand why we believe in monogamy, see it for what it is, and change our attitudes accordingly. For the secular community, monogamy has no foundation, no external arbiter and, so, no anchor in truth with a capital 'T'. In which case, prudence suggests, that we should take advantage of "truth's" new found pliability. And in understanding that the adoption of a religious answer to what is now a secular question no longer runs parallel with the goal of happiness, and its vehicle of Reason, we can start to evict monogamy from the house of virtue. This will help enable us to condition future generations for healthier, more stable, happier relationships instead of equipping our youngsters for mental anguish, guilt and failure. Removing present re-enforced givens, with generational turnover, will bring about greater harmony between what we think and how we behave. Instead of the inevitable battle to suppress what we really, deep down, think about our relationships, in the quest for happiness, we will allow ourselves to own, not deny our innermost feelings because they will not be any different to our public feelings.

The key then to any such restoration of parity to what is promised and what is done is to agree to remove fidelity as a central plank of the marriage commitment and re-define its value in line with the principle of finding the mean between excess and deficiency. This, however, must run in unison with a programme of educating future children. In this way we can attempt to plant security for insecurity, love for jealousy and establish happiness as a genuine goal of marriage. And it is in this context of necessity for change that the following two chapters will develop.

Chapter Three

The Retrieval of the Romantic State

'For a dreamer can only find his way by the moonlight, and his punishment is that he sees the dawn before the rest of the world.'

(Oscar Wilde)

In the opening two chapters I have argued that monogamy as a virtue should be founded in "Moderation Theory" and not in fanaticism. In the next two chapters I want to explore two further themes that support what I see as the necessary shift of emphasis from 'Faithfulness' to 'Loyalty' as the grounding for longevity and contentment. This chapter addresses the need to emancipate Romance from the state of love and to recognize it as a self-contained state. Incorporated in this need for 'independence', is the additional necessity to retrieve what is rightfully the property of romance from lust, as well as the severing of the artificial link between romance and youth. The second theme (which is not unrelated to the former) that will be discussed in chapter four is the liberation of the unique individual from the abstract notion of "Relationship" coupled with a positive acceptance of the fact that very few of us ever marry our emotional mirror.

Love, Sex, Youth and the retrieval of the Romantic State

In the last chapter, we looked at 'Love' in the context of its relationship with monogamy. There, monogamy's monopoly of the loving relationship was shown to be highly questionable. Therefore, in the spirit of tolerance to other ideas, at most, it should be seen as *a* face of love and not *the* face of love. Love, has a multitude of faces, and while we might be able to recognise them, perhaps we know the names of none of them. Thus, it is safer to hold that 'real' love remains pure only when it remains uncommercialised by language and is defined by individual actions appropriate to individual circumstance. Language can only serve to make love conditional to the definition of the words used to describe it, and as love is the greatest master of paradox, it will always outwit and out-dignify the pretensions of definition. The state of Romance, on the other hand, is less complex, (or less 'hidden' from language) and is both describable and definable.

The buzz of that "Just met" feeling, the verbal and non-verbal sparring, and those wonderful first touches are narcotic by nature and in being so, romance is often mistaken for love. The fundamental importance of the Romantic State, however, lies outside of the aesthetic. Its true value lies in its ability to facilitate the complete freedom to be yourself [again] in what you think and what you say and how you dress and how you act. However transient a phase this may be, it provides a 'space' to reveal and explore areas of one's personality that the common notion of Relationship conceals, and what makes this 'space' unique, is that it is bereft of the boredom and loneliness that accompanies the freedom of being single. Our problem though, is that Romance as a state is a concept not seen as independent and has been mentally annexed by three other categories, namely love, youth and sex (or lust). In this blurring of the genuinely romantic, with the concepts of love, sexual freedom or youth, we overlook the Romantic State as a state in itself when discussing relationships and advocating the prescription of monogamy. Therefore, the link between infidelities and an overwhelming desire or need for romance is missed. I shall now, briefly, look at each in turn and then outline the ramifications of an independent Romantic State for the prescription of monogamy as the foundation of long-term relationships.

Love

The tendency to confuse romance and love as two parts of the same emotion and/or action denies Romance exclusivity as a potent emotional state. Romance should not be viewed as a relatively short lasting prelude to a longer 'more serious' relationship. It is in fact a 'serious' state in its own right and is not merely the exciting start of a loving relationship. Although is *does* provide that function, to see that *as* its function, is to misunderstand and underestimate the significance of the Romantic State. To put it another way, the two emotions of love and romance are a Crocodile and an Alligator. They look the same but they do not mate with each other. Therefore, romance is not merely the chrysalis stage of love, and to see them as intrinsically connected is a mistake. In turn, this closes doors to potential areas of self-exploration and, thus, can help to stifle potential personal development.

Youth

The second common idea is that romance is essentially for the young and not the business of those with responsibilities. It is, therefore, too easily dismissed as the property of adolescence. This sentiment is characterised in comments such as " He makes me feel like I'm eighteen again", or "I haven't felt like this since I was a kid". The reason people say these things, when finding themselves in new romances after separation from long-term partners, is not because romance is part of the experience of youth but simply because they were a youth when they last felt like that. Far from being immature or a 'fixed' phase within the maturation process, romance has an essential facilitating role to play in our *continual* development and in keeping ourselves *ourselves*.

Lust

Thirdly, in terms of perception, being 'unfaithful' is more often than not seen by 'wronged parties', not in terms of the development of an individual, but an excuse for sex. No doubt the natural physical urge for new sexual partners has currency as an explanatory tool where infidelity is concerned. After all who would watch a porn film they had seen before one they had not? However, the desire for 'fresh flesh' for the desperate want of a better expression cannot and does not explain infidelity alone. It is, for the most part, only part of a bigger more powerful desire for romance.

At this point, it is worth underlining that what we are discussing is long-term adult relationships ensconced in the tedium of responsibility and trials of everyday existence. We are not talking about the kids in a sweet shop mentality that characterises teenage life, or for that matter, the lifestyles that are associated with glamour professions such as the arts. Therefore, I am not in the business of advocating constant infidelity and/or condoning a constant search for kicks. It is more a case of understanding why we do what we actually do in reality, which is out of sync with what we are obliged to feel or think. It is that understanding which is fundamental if we are to start responding to the increasing inevitability of adultery in a measured and appropriate manner. Secondly, any vulgarity attached to the above is deliberate, as if it is deemed so, then that can only lend support to my argument that infidelity is not just about a 'sordid' pursuit of lust. For if a reader finds the terminology inappropriate to describe a relationship they have had outside their marriage then their motivation must have been something more than just sex, which I suggest is an inherent necessity for romance. After all, a loving marriage is more than capable of incorporating sex defined as lust as part of a couples overall repertoire of love making. Prostitution, is of course, another traditional provision of just sex, even if some of its clientele are looking for services not provided such as company, care and friendship. And as already said; pure sexual attraction does have a role in extramarital relationships. However, it is only romance that can provide the liberation that comes with the "Just met" scenario and in that context, arguably, the role of the sexual act is not that important. So, where explanations of infidelity are concerned, we have to be suspicious of the simplistic "I had sex with them but I make love to you" cliché. The fact is monogamy, and its admirers, (leaving aside the notion of negative pragmatism discussed in chapter two), are basically saying that what I *have* is superior to something outside of the marriage. Given the context of fidelity, that could mean one of two things. Monogamy as opposed to polygamy or open marriages, for example, only differs from other systems in the number of sexual partners. It is frankly pure arrogance to see other forms of marital structure as somehow less loving or of inferior all round quality. Therefore, either the loving act itself is superior or the overall quality of the relationship is not worth jeopardising for any dubious short-term satisfaction. Therefore, effectively both have, on the surface at any rate, the assumption that the sexual act is all that is involved. The first implies that sex is better at home and the second implies that it is not worth losing a good relationship over sex. However, as romance is mistakenly connected to love and therefore strong feelings of attachment, we tend to write off indiscretions as "just sex" and nothing "serious" in order not to justify but to try to lessen the impact of infidelity. Yet, in doing so, we help to confine romance to nothing more than the initial stage of love. In turn, infidelity is generally only seen in either of two ways. Firstly, purely in sexual terms, which by definition will damage, if not ruin a monogamous relationship, even if that relationship survives. Indiscretions may be forgiven but are never forgotten. Secondly, if infidelity is seen in terms of romance it is catastrophic because of the perception of an intrinsic link between romance and falling in love.

The romantic state

The recognition of independence of the Romantic State naturally has negative connotations for the prescription of monogamy. All the time romance is conceived in terms of love, youth and sex it proves a useful ally of monogamy. To confine romance to a simple facilitating role of enabling a loving relationship to start is convenient as the loving relationship once underway, according to the monogamist, manifests itself in a long monogamous relationship. Youth, is something to grow out of and therefore romance (in the sense I am defining it) has little place in responsible adult life and of course sex for the sake of sex is a vice and is to be frowned upon when conducted outside of the monogamous partnership. However, if the romantic emotion exists quite separately then it takes up a position in direct conflict with monogamy. And if romance is indeed a powerful developmental aid and a requirement of living a happy and fulfilled emotional existence then it becomes very difficult to square with the idea that monogamy is the corner stone of long-term relationships. Romance cannot ever be felt twice with the same person in a continuous relationship. Some things in life are once only scenarios. In the same way you are born only once and in males the voice breaks only once, the "Just met" aesthetic happens only once between two people. Second honeymoons, dressing up, flowers, meals, gifts and nostalgia done in the search for the "Just met" spark are doomed to failure; the absurd prescriptions of agony aunt and day time television morality. It treats romance with little respect and only as a one off precursor to something "more serious" and if the apologists for monogamy have their way; once a long-term relationship is embarked upon, the Romantic State is never to be experienced again. The monogamous marriage can then be seen as a state of romance in remission, and therefore, it is bound to foment conflict between the need for romance on the one hand and the vow of fidelity on the other.

Romance

To illustrate the importance of romance, think of it in this way. When our health is suddenly taken away from us the simple things in life very quickly take on their 'proper' status. Denied the freedom and privileges that health bestows, and lying in a hospital bed, day-to-day life acquires a certain magical quality. Catching a train or a bus, going for a walk or going to the pub for a drink are, all of a sudden, things we would give anything to be able to do. Experiencing this emotion gives us an insight into the power of the Romantic State and its "Just met" aesthetic. Romance lifts the mundane to exactly those heights. A monotonous train journey with someone recently met is anything but monotonous: it is fantastic. Twelve years of marriage does not and cannot restore a sense of quality to everydayness. The reason for this, of course, is that once our 'health' is restored to us, it is not long before the simple things appear once again simple, everyday, and in their monotony are taken for granted.

Romance, in all its subtlety, can be seen as having two basic qualities: the aesthetic and the developmental. The aesthetic, described above, is the cataract operation that allows us to view our life differently, and in doing so, it provides the space for the developmental. Who we are is all too often concealed if not lost or forgotten in who and what our partners believe or desire us to be. The present long-term monogamous structure can actively discourage personal development especially if any such development is seen by partners as going against the demands of Relationship or 'togetherness'. Therefore, it is not uncommon for there to be a tendency to knock our partner's ideas, thoughts, plans, or for that matter, achievements. One of the attractions of the "Just met" scenario, then, is that you can speak freely without (whether deliberate or not) anecdotal interruption from someone who invokes your past, or their knowledge of you, somehow undermining or devaluing what you are saying. In short, the Romantic State encourages development because it does not fall prey to the restraining cynicism of familiarity. "New" people view us differently and encourage personality development "old" people often have the habit of keeping us within the limitations of whom they 'know' us to be. This implicit understanding of each other reduces conversation as we can predict our partner's responses which will be, more often than not, suspicious if not simply negative to ideas and plans for personal experience, development and change.

Oscar Wilde in his *De Profundis* wrote that 'the bond of all companionship, whether in marriage or friendship, is conversation'. A lot of couples of a few years and beyond find it very difficult to manage a conversation and a drink by themselves in a Pub. Once away from the domestic stimuli of the home, they struggle almost embarrassingly for meaningful conversation. They can have a drink but not a conversation. A couple engaged in the Romantic State sitting at another table have no such problems. Ideas, laughter and the genuine experience of individuality provide a damming contrast to the deafening silence of familiarity. Imagine a restaurant full of long-term couples on Valentines Night. Assuming they were all of comparable looks, if they really wanted a romantic evening all the women should get up and move around one table. The restaurant would quickly become a hive of chatter, flattery, flirtation, and born again individuals.

Humour apart, the urge for romance is a factor rarely taken into proper consideration and sooner or later, when ignored, [it] will disturb the smooth running of the long-term relationship. Which married person does not feel a pang of envy when a single friend of theirs rings up and tells them they have got a new man or women? This envy probably only being placated by the 'new recruit' not 'matching up' (in our eyes) to our own partner. Nostalgic conversations such as "Tell me about when you first met me" or "do you remember when we did this or that" are the 'tell tell' signs of a couple admitting they are in need of romance, even if they do not consciously know it. I would also propose that some marriages are in themselves an unconscious attempt on behalf of a long-term couple to recapture the romantic. "Maybe if we get married that will make us feel how we used to in the early days". It could be that even children are sometimes undertaken in a forlorn attempt to feel the feelings that only the "Just met" can provide. The error, then, of underestimating the pull of romance, and its attempted suppression, is another problematic in the quest for marriage characterised by longevity and happiness. Implicit in the monogamous marriage is the denial of romance being anything more than a phase in life, to be felt no more once married. The irony of the marriage day being that on the supposedly most romantic day of all, one agrees never to feel romance again. This leaves the married couple in the dilemma that whilst to commit adultery be a sin, not to, is a tragedy.

The sacrifice of romance, then, defined in terms of its aesthetic and developmental properties, is an additional tension to the irrational nature of the sacrifice involved in secular monogamy, as outlined in the first two chapters. Therefore, when explaining the disparity between what we actually do in practice with what we explicitly agree to do in theory, [it] is another factor overlooked, by bland platitudes of value restoration of the sort favoured by the traditionalist fraternity. If we are to, genuinely, confront our predicament of 'short-term' long-term relationships and stave off the onslaught of serial monogamy and, in turn, a circus of parenthood, the adoption of more open and honest values is paramount. As I have stated, a more open and honest approach to our values would be to force monogamy to find its virtue on the virtuous mean between excess and deficiency. We would then, no doubt, present ourselves with a new set of uncomfortable and difficult problems. However, the difference being these problems would be solvable as they stem, for the most part from education and custom and not essential human requirement. Whereas, at present, essential human requirement in terms of happiness or living as opposed to existing is asked to give way to custom, we would have a situation where custom is asked to give way to the pursuit of fundamental human good. The failure of Reason to provide absolutes and the misplaced optimism of the enlightenment to establish truth outside of the irrational, means secular man and secular monogamist must understand that we make up the rules. Once we establish autonomy of authority, then, in this context, our problem becomes one of controlling the negative emotions that we feel when our partners behave in a way that we disapprove of, despite the fact that we are perfectly prepared to do the same. So, instead of custom based in the old reassurances of absolutes, custom should be based in our new

found self-reliance. The task then in accepting the independence of the Romantic State is one of attuning
attitudes in line with contentment or happiness imperatives. Or, to put it another way, stop conditioning to
negative sets of emotions, namely pride, jealousy and fear
in the name of virtue and eternal notions of what is right,
and replace it with education centered on happiness,
stability, loyalty and honesty. Thus, the virtue of
'monogamy in moderation' would be a value of the future
and not the past or atemporal. However, a pragmatist
approach will only come to fruition in future generations
if our present one can find within them the humility to
accept what they have already agreed to is actually wrong
and begin to teach our children something closer to
reality. In this way our unsatisfactory present can be
replaced with a more satisfactory future.

Romance in Moderation: The practical problems?

The first objection to the actual practice of accepting the
Romantic State as separate from love and a necessary part
of personal development would be the potential problem
of separation. When one partner enters into a romance
with someone else what is to stop them liking the other
person more than the person they are having a long-term
relationship with? Why won't they go off with the new
partner just as they do frequently in the present state of
affairs (if you will excuse the pun)?

   This is, of course, perfectly possible; to suggest that it is
not going to happen would be ridiculous. Nonetheless, I
think it is less likely than under the current system of
monogamy for four reasons. Firstly, the basic recognition

of romance as a positive, vitalising state for a human life would enable people to understand more fully how they *actually* feel given these new set of circumstances. By this I mean, instead of their new romantic state instigating a situation where an individual thinks they have "fallen in love" or the new person they have met, makes them feel different, in a positive way over and above their long-term partner, they would be better positioned to see it for exactly what it is. Our awareness would be such that we would see romance as a developmental tool and as 'additional' to what we have already, and not as a replacement. They would also be fully aware of the fact that the new feelings will not last and will turn into what they already have. Secondly, and crucially, without the pretext of monogamy people are more likely to embark on long-term relationships with people they find attractive but have more in common with. Whatever the voice of idealism says, monogamy makes the 'looks' factor too much of an issue when it comes to choosing partners for life. I fully accept this is probably an accusation generally better aimed at men but this is exactly what men do. And even when a man makes a more sensible choice not predominately based on looks but personality, with monogamy in situe, his 'superior' decision will often be plagued by doubt. So if, without the vow of fidelity, more appropriate partners are found, when the Romantic State is entered into and seen for what it is and will eventually become, the desire to leave our relationships will be far less than at present. Thirdly, with the notion of adultery replaced with the demands of happiness and unconditional love, guilt in turn will have less of a role to play. The guilt attached to affairs often pressurises the need for premature and uninformed decisions. The guilt and stigma attached to 'cheating' tempts premature separation and irrevocable damage. The fourth argument as to why entering into occasional romantic relationships alongside a long-term commitment will not be the threat to the stability of relationships that it is at present, is that 'Romances' will be exploring relatively small areas of our personalities; liberating only the nuances of our thoughts, passions, needs and desires. This idea will be discussed later. However, it is worth mentioning here as it is another powerful reason why people will not be tempted to turn a romance into a chore. Who would give up the keys to a mansion to live in a tiny cottage overlooking a loch in Scotland? We would all probably like to spend a two-week holiday there but we would not really want to live there, especially when we have had our holiday. However, this will be discussed more fully later.

A second practical problem of this system is the question of jealousy. In chapter two I argued the emotion of jealousy like greed and aggression is an emotion that, given the right education, can be controlled. Even if only in the sense that individuals self- regulate to the norms of social interaction. After all there are successful open relationships where individuals do control their jealousy. They are not freaks; they have just thought about it and let reason and honesty take a central role in educating their emotional reflexes. Thus atavism gives way to dignity, and mutual sacrifice in subordination to jealousy and insecurity gives way to development. If we could inject the notion that romance was a blessing necessary to living full and complete lives and not be seen as a threat, we could begin to build a culture where pettiness and drudgery would have a diminished role in day to day domesticity. However, this is the long-term goal of slow and incremental changing of attitudes and would take generational turnover to come to fruition.

A third perceived problem could be when a 'married' person enters into a relationship with a single person. It could be argued that the person who is single will be exposed to having their emotions toyed with and could easily end up getting hurt. There is a genuine distinction to be made between two 'married' people entering into a relationship both understanding that they are experiencing romance and expecting nothing more and two 'available' people whose relationship could develop into something more permanent. However, when there is a relationship between someone who is not 'available' and someone who is, this could be problematic. Obviously, this situation is not uncommon in the system we already have. Many 'available' people are kept on the sidelines in the hope that their lover will eventually leave their spouse. However, arguably this situation is perpetuated by the notion that romance and love are part of the same emotion. The married person continues in the belief that they "love them both, but in different ways" yet is perhaps more often than not failing to recognise that one is about love, and the other is about romance. While, the single person is expecting that the romance will develop into something more serious, namely love. However, romance by definition is finite and with the awareness raised both parties would be fully aware of this fact at the beginning. Added to the premise of honesty outlined in chapter two, any single person involved with an 'attached individual' will understand they are experiencing a finite emotion and a finite relationship instead of being fed lies and half truths. Prolonged enforced single life taxes even the most independent and strong personalities. In a world designed for couples it is not easy to feel "normal" when finding oneself seemingly unable to fit the bill as far as the way one is perceived. Embarrassment is never too far away when lovers, sex, marriage, relationships, affairs, and one night stands respectively, form a fair old chunk of conversations in any circles. I think there is a definite unspoken 'them' and 'us' atmosphere attached to long-term coupledom and long-term singledom. Indeed, fear of singledom is why a lot of unhappy people in relationships only leave them once a new suitor has been found. Frankly, it is easier to get a job from a job and if you are long-term unemployed the false perception of your unsuitability is partly lent authority by your lack of confidence and protection mechanisms of ambivalence. It is much easier to show a bit of vulnerability when your confidence is still intact, it is charming as opposed to 'sad'. A Romantic State for a single person based on honesty could be extremely valuable in terms of self-confidence and self-respect which helps keep a natural quality to their associations with the opposite sex partners which in turn makes them more attractive upon meeting other 'available' potential partners. Thus, mutually beneficial romances could be conducted minus the negative aspects associated with this sort of behaviour as it is presently enacted.

Conclusion

This may all be the folly of a man who cannot commit himself. However, that very charge is just as poignant if the monogamist would just take a look in the mirror. In general the monogamous individual cannot commit either. They stay in a relationship until they do not want to anymore and then they move on. They use the pejorative vocabulary monogamy covets, "Cheating", "affairs" or "whores", "bastards" and "slags" etc. until they have their own affair. 'Monogamous' couples are now splitting up and getting divorced in ever increasing numbers and, I suggest, it is in part down to the desire for someone new or in other words, a search for romance. Perhaps the only difference between the author and the monogamist is that whilst we are both dreamers, this dreamer at least, 'looks before he leaps'.

The persistent and unwavering tacit support for monogamy inevitably means the young simply have to find out for themselves that the myths shrouding the 'loving monogamous relationship' are just that, myths. The support for monogamy, in all its grandiose self-importance, as the 'true' follower of virtue, and the sole owner of a unique, ubiquitous therapeutic message maintains an absurd status quo. Stubborn social and cultural values combined with mass submission to jealousy, fear and pride have a direct causal relationship to the underlying discontent that characterises the western relationship leaving us in a constant cycle of failure, guilt and hurt. However, the modern consequences of this cycle have changed with prevalent separation and serial monogamy having replaced the silent suffering, behind the closed doors of protocol. The modern consensus of serial monogamy is in itself nothing more than a fashionable camouflage of the fact that many are not prepared to commit to the values they say they have. Or put another way; they are, but only for as long as it suits them to do so. Whilst the former is preferable on an individual basis, socially, in terms of its emotional and financial cost, it is not. To borrow and adjust Marx's famous phrase monogamy 'digs its own grave' as it creates the environment for its own destruction and perpetuates and encourages selfishness: in that we demand our partner's fidelity despite our own indiscretions or we stay faithful until we want to leave (directly because we have to be faithful), either leaving or taking the children with us. The real irony of all this is that only in monogamy is the concept of sharing considered selfish. This must be attributed to the unilateral nature of infidelity under the roof of monogamy. Parents, teachers and politicians and of course partners who continue to preach monogamy as the fundamental corner stone of the loving relationship leave our children to instability and uncertainty in childhood and naiveté as to what it means to be in a relationship as an adult.

My final thought in this chapter, is this: when we do separate from our long-term partners we see them in a completely different light. We see them as a person and not as part of ourselves. We also find them more attractive than prior to the separation. We see them in the 'lost light' which is similar to the 'to be gained light' that we originally see them upon meeting them. If we were to accept the need for romance when embarking on a relationship from the outset, it is possible that we will see the person we love in the light of 'to be gained' and 'not to be lost' rather than the fading light of 'we have'. And in this way we will have what we love and keep what we first met and, thereafter, fell in love with.

Chapter Four

The Individual, Expansion and Development, not Invasion and Occupation

'It is from having what we desire that we are happy – not from having what others think desirable.'

(Rochefoucauld)

Uniqueness of the individual

The second theme I want to address as to why monogamy would be better to find its virtue at the point of balance between excess and deficiency, and not in the dogmatic or the fanatical, is in the notion of the primacy of the individual. At present our love is partner orientated. However, this seemingly selfless proposition is in fact negative for it *demands* sacrifice and does not earn it. The expectation that one's spouse should conform to a necessary criteria in the name of the 'God' of compromise perverts the nature of sacrifice as it removes the personal and the voluntary and replaces it with the impersonal and involuntary. The affect of this means not only do we live unhealthily well within the perimeters of our full potential both actively and emotionally but we are at the same time denied any solace that authentic altruism may provide. We should be very suspicious of "Relationships are all about compromise", which is the usual justification for the unwholesome amalgamation of two people into a manufactured 'one'.

I shall now try to elucidate what I mean by sacrifice being impersonal and involuntary and the unhealthy drive to oneness that it helps to co-ordinate. The Danish philosopher Kierkeguaard, in his criticism of what he saw as personal opinion becoming no more than the repetition of public opinion, saw the human as rapidly becoming a 'species of ventriloquism'. Patrick Gardiner sums up Kierkeguaard's observation as follows.

'Rather than confront the reality that everyone is finally accountable to himself (or herself) for his life, character, and outlook, they take refuge in a depersonalised realm of rarified ideas and doctrines'. (OUP 1988 p. 36)

When it comes to relationships I suggest the rarified doctrines of "give and take" and "compromise" have lost any genuine autonomy and therefore, in this case, value. This is so for two reasons. Firstly, they do not apply to the romantic and sexual requirements of couples, only to the non-sexual arenas of everyday communal living. This is because of the rarified doctrine of monogamy forbids it such. Notions of compromise clearly play a supportive role to the notion of monogamy, as compromise, cannot be invoked by an individual in a relationship to challenge the idea of monogamy. Therefore, the notion of compromise has already been doctored by public opinion before the principle is called on by any individual.

Secondly, the notion of Relationship itself is a mistake and merely the manifestation of mass conformity to what 'one' *should* say and how 'one' *should* act in a 'relationship'.

So compromise is conducted for the sake of, and against a backdrop of, how 'one' *should* act in a relationship. Individual thought in these matters is usually seen as selfish precisely because in terms of Relationship it does not fit the bill. However, to think in this way must presume that somewhere there exists, the 'perfect relationship' that provides an external measure with which to judge our partner's behaviour by. Obviously, there is no such thing as Relationship existing independently of any *two people*. It is not possible to buy a left shoe and a right shoe *and* a pair of shoes. The right and the left shoe *are* the pair of shoes. In the same way you cannot have one person and another person *and* a relationship; the two people *are* the relationship. However, despite the uniqueness of personality and individual preference, the problems of long-term relationships are all too similar, if not ubiquitous, in nature. This is due to the predominance of 'public' opinion being voiced over and above the recognition of individual need and thus at the expense of authentic individual opinion.

My suggestion then is this; society has made its own monster. Frankenstein-style, we have created a crude hybrid of a few basic ideas and called it 'A Relationship' and then thrown this onto the infinite possibilities of relationships, if centered on private responsibility for thought. The result is that we have a culture of "You shouldn't do this or that... because remember I didn't do this or that...", all 'virtuously' done in deference to the almighty Relationship, and in preference to "You should do this or that" because you are an individual and "I should do this or that" because I am an individual and "we should accept each other's actions and thoughts" because "we *are* the relationship". In short, relationships may well be essentially all about compromise, but not compromise in deference to a public conception of what it means to be in a Relationship. At present, give and take and compromise lead to 'Inward compromise' characterised by a landscape of curtailing behaviour in pursuit of relationship maintenance. "You stop doing this and I will stop doing and/or desiring this or that", is a very simplistic analysis of the gradual balding of the personality that pervades the long-term commitment. The eventual result of this is an uneasy 'oneness', that 'oneness' being the sum of what has not been given away in the name of Relationship. We have the bread, but all the toppings are gone.

Trying to make two people a united 'one' is characterised by the abuse of apology. People, always apologising to their partners for not giving way to Relationship, in other words for not needlessly sacrificing any given behaviour or beliefs, and privately thinking "what's the big deal". But they kowtow generally persuaded their behaviour failed in terms of Relationship, even if it is merely a conciliatory gesture in the name of a quiet life. The innocent must apologise to the court for their misdeed. The fact that the court represents something that does not actually exist is quietly forgotten. In contrast to when the relationship was in its infancy or its "Just met" stage, where far greater respect is afforded to individuals where tolerance reigns and interest is the only thing unwittingly being maintained.

The transition from romance or the "good bit" as it is often rather tellingly referred to, to the "serious bit", as it is also rather tellingly referred to, is a mystery to most of us. It happens but few of us can actually pin point exactly when. One day we just seem to be aware things are not the same as they used to be, and have not been for a period of time. For the purposes of identification, I think it useful to break this transition into two parts: the behavioural and the sexual. The sexual transition is inevitable. The sensation of touching someone new can never be truly revisited once it has gone. However, the love making between two people more often than not gets better. It does not have to become a chore or boring. Nevertheless, love making normally drops off in most relationships from the comparatively frenzied action of "Just met". The key to this, however, possibly lies in staving off the behavioural transition.

The behavioural transition is by no means such a certainty as the sexual transition, but ironically, we seem to be more concerned at keeping the 'sexual' transition at bay whilst almost oblivious to the behavioural change that is occurring simultaneously. Indeed, the behavioural change may ironically, in some cases, even be motivated by the desire to keep the romantic spark alive. Albeit, be in the name of 'closeness', 'oneness' is nonetheless creeping in subsuming the individual into the all-encompassing web of the relationship. However, checking the behavioural transition arguably would help keep the attraction, which fires the sexual desire. Less attention to 'oneness' and more to individuality is the very attraction of romance. In short, noticing the fact that romance has given way to familiarity and Relationship is not just one of those little curiosities and something that "just happens". This event is part and parcel of the territory that goes with monogamy, in that the commanding of individuals to 'oneness' is endemic. So to a large extent we 'let' this transition happen in part due to the primacy given to the expectations and assumptions of the 'public' relationship and not the 'private'. We do this over and above what it is to be a person 'in our own right'? The transition from romance to relationship could then be summarised as such: individual behaviour goes from being acceptable and intriguing in the Romantic State, to selfish in the relationship. Then, with the onset of 'selfishness' and the call to selflessness, the capitulation of the individual to the necessarily petty nature of much relationship maintenance is all too prevalent. The silent war conducted is fought with 'public opinion' inoculating us from its bloodshed. Partner's desires assemble in the territories of behaviour we want to change in each other. And the "you have me now" and "I am more important" mentality starts to wage war seizing individuality and turning it into 'togetherness'. Our response is not to protect these territories of behaviour and thought, no task forces are dispatched; only surrender flags. Chunks of the sovereign individual are handed over for nothing and without a fight. Change, once embraced, can never be altered without an argument, because this is now 'occupied land' and is seen very much in that light. (Give up smoking and try starting again without an argument. Have a cigarette when you have split up and are discussing your problems and possible reconciliation and there will be no argument).

If the territory is never occupied then behaviour is not *replaced* by a partner's ideas and needs. It is important that our partner's wishes and ideas are an *addition* to us as an individual and, in this way, the nature of compromise is in an outward not inward fashion. Thus, Relationship is geared to the individuals who *make it* and a forum for security and "expansion" not security via "invasion" and "occupation". To opt for security through invasion and surrender is to pay into a pension of regret and, I think, privately we are all too aware of this, leaving us dwelling in the cold doubt, somewhere between the fear of losing our security and the fear of regret. In short, transition, in the spirit of oneness, is characterised by the change in the nature of compromise. This change precipitates the amalgamation of the two into a sense of oneness, which dominates the vast majority of decision making, if an argument is to be avoided. A sense of duty or obligation not to do what is individually willed hangs like a dark cloud, ensuring that our experience is the mediocrity of 'inward compromise', and living well within ourselves. Furthermore, as a result of 'togetherness', won in the name of Relationship, many of us are in love with projections of what they *think* our partners *are*, namely what is left standing after the 'replacement war', but not who they *actually are*. This illusion is corroborated and further reinforced by a failure of honesty and, in this way, individual behaviour is made clandestine; the lie becomes the essential facilitator of individual action. Thus, the elevation of deceit becomes an important tool in relationship maintenance.

We have a choice; so called 'security in occupation and oneness' or 'security in individuality, respect and development'. The former has been tried tested and failed. Our task then, if we are to choose the latter, is to accept the uniqueness of the individual and use the notion of Relationship as a celebration of individualism and the joining of the two, not a celebration of sacrifice, and the forming of the one. However, to do this, it is imperative to recognise the uniqueness of the individual, and accept we cannot and do not marry our soul mirror and most importantly accept this within, not outside, the sexual context. The perfect relationship in its public manifestation is the concealment of what has been lost to the clandestine world of individuality facilitated through deception, assuming it is still visible and not lost to the individual her/himself. As I see it, we have a dilemma when entering a relationship. Do I live *all* of me or *some* of me? This is what I call the "sixty-percent question". The figure is totally an arbitrary one meaning an agreeable amount of compatibility is the best that can be hoped for. If you decide not to live 60% but attempt 100% of who you are; then, the other 40% will have to be explored through other people. Monogamy, therefore, is an inappropriate system. Whilst, monogamy relies for its continuation on clandestine behaviour, lies and imperatives of non-detection, it is a system that generally fails, and only 'succeeds' for the most part where the lie is rewarded. Here, I think it important to clarify I am not saying everyone commits adultery (although a great deal more do, or would like to, than care to admit it). I am saying that very few relationships thrive in terms of honesty. We, therefore, endorse a system that restricts love to illusion; the illusion of loving not what we 'have' but what we 'want' to have. Clandestine action breeds contempt in both camps, actions hidden from the 'relationship' are deemed out of line with the illusion the 'wronged' partner loves, and the perpetrator resents the fact that his or her behaviour cannot be loved as part of who they are. Deception then, whether successful or not, will always undermine the goal of happiness because the long-term relationship, based on inward compromise, breeds resentment out of prolonged containment.

However, if we accept that the other 40% of ourselves, which, we pursue at present under cover of illusion and deception (if at all), should be lived without apology, then the vow of monogamy and its ties to 'real' love must be abandoned. If we embrace the reality of a 'limited multiplicity' of partners being the essence of self-fulfillment and the genuine expression of 'real' love, ironically the goal of longevity, stability, love and happiness will more likely be found. To do this we need to re-articulate what it *is* we agree to do. With the severing of monogamy from love and security, infidelity loses its status as a vice and can find its virtue in the common sense of moderation theory. Thus, the supernatural, myth and silliness that characterises much of the expectation of monogamy, can be allowed to rest peacefully with other dead virtues. All of which died of natural secular causes once they had outlived contemporary usefulness.

The omission of the monogamy vow will facilitate a better system of partner selection. This, in turn, will provide a more satisfactory platform from which to live 100% of ones potential in the spheres of love, the romantic, and the sexual. There is a genuine, if somewhat repugnant argument, that in many cases partner choosing is reduced to a single issue, namely attractiveness. I, personally, will not hide behind the language of 'shallowness' and 'immaturity' and the refuge such language provides to all those who 'lost' when it came to finding and getting the looks they initially desired. Nobody, would happily accept their partner (whose 'personality' they love) being temporarily removed from them and returned to them in an 'uglier' form. And frankly, more sensible choices, not guided by looks, do very well if they honestly avoid the occasional internal dialogue of doubt. It is easy to duck the 'looks' factor, but to play it down in any such discussion in observance to the 'wouldn't it be nice if this was true' school of honesty, is counter-

productive. Honesty is the one of the few empirical meas-
ures we have to measure the emotions with, and therefore,
I exercise mine and any objectivity is found in the recognition of the reader. In turn the broader the recognition the
greater the objectivity, if after honest consideration, there
is indeed any recognition. It is a truism that with age looks
are less important, but is that really the case? Is it not a
case of having simply to be more realistic in our goals as
we age? No doubt, people do mature and look for other
qualities outside of looks, but it is always looks that will
first catch our attention. Obviously, older people generally avoid going out with the beauty of youth because
they cannot be bothered to with the immaturity and
lifestyles attached. However, looks are still very important
albeit relative to their circumstance. At any rate, this is a
question that all too often is the victim of public opinion
of what *should be* the case and never very honestly
discussed. However, somewhat in contradiction, let us
agree that cynicism has the better of me and people do
come to the conclusion that looks are not particularly relevant when it comes to partner choosing. They normally
arrive at this conclusion through having already made the
mistake of choosing partners based on attractiveness.

Without the insistence of monogamy, partner choosing
would then be more compatible with long-term stability
for two reasons. Firstly, the couple would be better friends
because they would have more in common and a greater
understanding of each other's needs. Secondly, this better
companionship would prove essential when embarking
on the sort of perception changes and outward compromise that I am advocating. What I am suggesting is that
we should marry our sixty-percent and make up the rest
of our needs and desires through outward compromise

and expansion from within the relationship and intermittent 'Romantic States' from without. The important thing to realise is that if we marry 60% (within the context of a relationship based on moderation theory) we will stop leaving our partners for those who are offering the opportunity to explore small areas of ourselves; areas that have been, hitherto, either sacrificed or forced underground by the movement of 'oneness' and inward compromise. A small illustration of what I mean is this; a woman may very well hold dear a romantic trip to the theatre. However, her partner does not like the theatre very much. He thinks it has snobbish overtones and feels much more at home with the casual nature of the cinema. Early on in the relationship the woman does not mind that she does not go to the theatre, or if she does go, it is with a friend or mother or whatever. This "go with someone else" mentality, is both right and wrong. However, it is wrong because under monogamous authority, the "someone else" by definition cannot provide the very experience that is desired. Namely, she wants a *romantic* trip to the theatre not a trip to the theatre. But is it right in that someone else can and should fulfill this desire, or should it be a victim of the compromise inward approach to love? The problem with sacrifice is that with prolonged abstinence, the quality of life denied grows from a nominal percentage of one's romantic personality to a requirement all out of proportion with its status. Dissatisfactions grow like a cancer until what once was a romantic 'side-show' has become a dangerous threat to a relationship. People end up meeting other people who are compatible with small areas of our romantic and sexual make-up, but are perceived to be much more suitable simply because the importance of these small nuances of desire have become so disproportionate. "Oh! Julian is wonderful he takes me to the theatre". Thus, in line with monogamy, people do the honest virtuous and dutiful thing and start painful and totally unnecessary separation procedures. Only to realise, after a relatively short period, that it has all been a mistake because Julian is not that great after all. Of course he is not because, once satisfied a few times, our 'theatre trip' assumes its rightful place in our romantic make up. Therefore in the '60% stakes' he is much more likely to be found wanting. However, the damage to the long-term relationship is done. This sort of behaviour happens at the moment but it is different for two main reasons. Firstly, we do not tend to pick the right partners under monogamy because men consider looks too important. Even if the claim that women do not is as valid as they say it is, it only takes the man to be doing this, to still create a certain artificiality to the relationship. Who the man appears to be is still motivated by his attraction to his partner and, in turn, who the woman is in love with, arguably, only exists as long as his attraction lasts. Once that has dulled then issues of compatibility are not so straight-forward so I would argue, the amount of 60% couples that exist is far less than there would be under a system based in moderation theory. This being the case, permanent separations are more likely as the drive to 'oneness' demands greater inward compromise, meaning to say in order to become a 'one' a couple individually have to suppress more of who they actually are. Therefore, there is more likelihood that others will have greater degrees of compatibility (outside of starved desire provision) when being instrumental in the break up of other people's long-term partnerships, thus, resulting in a greater number of permanent separations. Secondly, tying fidelity to love and trust and all things rosy in a relationship, results in the perceived necessity to leave one's partner. This may only occur once a clandestine affair has been discovered, and a disgruntled partner either leaves or demands a choice of "one or the other" being taken. Often, however, it is simply the consequence of the perceived virtue in strict fidelity and people feeling the necessity to end their relationship purely on the grounds that they have met someone else. Within the confines of a relationship founded in unconditional or 'real' love, the goals of living 100% of yourself, outward compromise and the expansion of each other, monogamy is not an essential expectation. Therefore, relationship casualties, whether in terms of actual permanent separation or the happiness shortfall of those that survive temporary 'separations', will be proportionately limited.

Living 100% of who we are, or at least attempting to, should be our goal for our partner; anything short represents a tourist approach to love. Relationships, in order to be authentic must be about the secure environment for the exploration of two very separate individuals. If demands *are* made upon the other, it should be in the spirit of expansion of the others personality and experience, and not a policy of replacement of behaviour in the quest for security and oneness. Much of the time, individual exploration will have a symbiotic relationship with the expansion of your partner. This is because we do not meet mirrors of ourselves. Therefore, implicit in the goal of 100% living is the notion of "Qualified First Choice", and in turn the individual shouldering of responsibility as opposed to blaming your partner for acting irresponsibly and not in accordance with the demands of 'Relationship' and 'oneness'. In other words under the Pyramid Theory of Marriage, when she walks off with Julian for a romantic evening out and ends up having sex with him, it is not her fault but your own fault. She has not damaged the relationship due to not 'sticking to rules' because there are no rules of a Relationship because it does not actually exist outside of the two individuals that make it up. In addition, you had the first choice to take her to the theatre, you were fully aware of her desire but you did nothing about it. So, by doing so you declined to expand your sexual and romantic horizons. However, in declining to expand those personal horizons your partner is stifled from exploring and experiencing a 'known' desire and need in her. Therefore, a refusal to expand one's own sexual and romantic borders is indistinguishable from selfishness, unless there is an acceptance of personal responsibility and thus a genuinely benign tolerance of being 'substituted' in the overall cause of your partners happiness and life. However, it is important to understand that not every facet of exploration will be an invitation for [a partner's] expansion. This is why I used the term 'qualified' first choice because it must also be accepted that some things are beyond a partner, in that, as a partner you are not necessarily unwilling, merely unable, to provide it. Obviously, for there to be a genuine situation where love is *lived in* and not just visited, mutual reciprocation is of a premium if outward compromise is to work. Then, what might appear ridiculous to many now, may in time look as 'ridiculous' that the suggestion that women should not have to obey their husbands or people should be able to have sex and/or live together outside of marriage, would have appeared to people of our grandparents times.

Instead of small areas of stifled behaviour being

allowed to fester and grow disproportionately in importance, they would be 'lived' and left just in the same way
other interests are, when they are not unnaturally with-
held from us. This is an extremely important issue because
it highlights the natural behaviour that guides the realm
of friendships and its infinite superiority over the sexual
partnership. We all have a variety of friends, many who
serve different parts of our individuality. It is also true
that holding a party or gathering we tend to avoid, if
possible, too much integration of this plurality of friendship as, despite ourselves liking everybody, they probably
would not mix all that well. Friendships occur naturally
because they avoid to a large extent the 'commitment' and
'sacrifice' that jealousy and insecurity demands in the
name of 'real love' or Relationship. Friendships also work
in such a way as to highlight the somewhat farcical nature
of how we conduct our sexual relationships. For example,
if we want to go out to the pub or the cinema we will ring
up a friend and see if they want to go. It may well be our
best friend or to be more accurate, *one* of our best friends
as we do not have a problem with our best friends having
other best friends or for that matter friends and casual
acquaintances in general. The point being, if they for some
reason do not want to participate in whatever the social
occasion being offered, we simply ring someone else up.
We certainly do not think, "Oh, they don't want to go to
the pub, so, I'd better not go". Imagine, meeting one of
your best friends, someone you have known for a long
time and who knows you really well. Someone you
discuss everything with. Sitting them quietly down and
uncomfortably explaining to them that you have recently
met another person who you have a good laugh with and
it is probably best all round if you stop seeing one another.

Totally ridiculous, yet this is the sort of thing we seem quite ready to do, albeit unhappily, in the name of monogamy, love, respect and of course the 'Relationship'. But "friendships are different to relationships" is the usual defence trotted out to excuse this rather embarrassing state of affairs. My response to this is twofold: firstly, they differ only in what is explicitly or implicitly agreed to in the first place and that agreement itself is normally one born of public opinion and not private opinion. Secondly, if you actually ask most couples who have been together for a long time what it is like or how they feel about it, they nearly always reply that it is "just like a really good friendship". If that is, indeed, the case then it appears to be a really good friendship minus the benefits of 'non-exclusivity' associated with other really good friendships, which, is a bit like being taxed at source without any of the benefits normally associated with being employed, such as holiday pay, sick pay and the in-built security of a proper procedure for dismissal.

Conclusion

The underlying point to this chapter is the liberation of the individual to be loved for who they are and not what they can be made. What they think, and what they want to experience should be respected, and respect in the end is built on the notion of freedom. However, the key to this freedom is that for the most part actually in practice, it will manifest itself not so much in the freedom to do what one wants and a complete change of behaviour, but a freedom from doubt. The making of the person then lies in giving your partner the freedom to see who they really are and not what they imagine themselves to be. Relationships suffer because what we *have* is seen as a hindrance to what we think we want for ourselves and, hence, doubt is allowed to cloud our judgement on what it is that would make us happy. The mental freedom to believe that we are in control of what we want to do and not hemmed in by Relationship is essential to freeing us to do willingly, what we, unwillingly, do now. In this way the voluntary and the personal is restored to action of sacrifice. However, with a greater respect for our partner's happiness and individuality, sacrifice will more often than not be 'outward' in nature and will lead to expansion, development and contentment within in the context of a relationship. In other words, what we have will be appreciated because we are free to want and do something else. Safe in the knowledge that quite often when we are unhappy with our lot and dream of the freedom associated with separation, granted our wish, we soon realise that we do not want it. The reality of freedom often teaches one that the world is not as accommodating to our wishes and desires as we imagined it to be so.

Conclusion

'Happiness comes from understanding one basic principle. Some things are within our control and some things
are not. Our body, wealth, fame, and social status are not
in our control. They are external to us and not our concern.
Our opinions, ambitions, desires and aversions are in our
control. We can change our inner character.'

(Epictetus)

There they go
out of their caves.
Into the sunlight of new experience.
Wife leaves husband
the changed are left behind.
Out they go, striding,
now walking, now wandering,
freedom heavy on their shoulders
across the darkening pastures
Into another cave.

(Dr. G Clifford)

In bringing my thoughts to an end, I consider it best to state
what I believe my purpose for writing them was in the first
instance. This book is not about prescribing some quick fix
theory that says if you follow this then all will be hunky
dory and the conundrum of how to live happily ever after

will all be a thing of the past. The argument I have sketched in here is intended merely to attack the complacency that underpins much of the language of Relationship. A more open and honest conversation is certainly required if we are to rid ourselves of the black and white and often hypocritical presumptions that are frankly unhelpful when addressing the problems of combining long-term family stability with personal goals of happiness. Obviously, this is just a theory and I anticipate that the reader, even if they are sympathetic to a lot of what has been written, will probably think that this is all very well, but in practice it will not work. However, it must also be understood that monogamy is itself, in the end, also is just a theory that in practice does not work. People, especially the younger generation, are increasingly becoming less prepared to commit their adult lives to any one person. In saying this, I acknowledge that there are couples who do but those are the exceptions and these exceptions themselves, if closely looked at, are probably far less than face value would suggest. How many happy monogamous couples can state that this is so because their infidelity went undetected? It is certainly an unarguable fact that there is a phenomenon where people willingly state that they would leave their partner if they found out that they had been unfaithful, yet would contemplate sleeping with someone else. It is also unarguable that present trends among the younger generation leave the future of the life-long or at least the 'family-long' relationship in jeopardy. Therefore, what this opinion merely proposes to do is outline a greater understanding of why infidelity sooner or later occurs. It does so without pretence in an attempt to, at least, bring about an honest debate as to the best way forward to try to protect the longevity of happy relationships.

The fact remains that people do have affairs and they, in turn, do have a direct causal relationship with separation. However, it is important to clarify that the suggestion to abandon monogamy does not mean a necessary mass philandering. In seeing it as a question of polar opposites is of little practical use and only helps to maintain the status quo of thought on the subject. So what I am suggesting is not so much a change of action but more a change of attitudes to what already happens and this change of attitude will be more likely brought about with a greater understanding of why we do what we do. The system may need overhauling but that does not mean I am advocating the sort of wholesale change simplistic revolutionary theories tend to demand. What is required is a system that both recognises the need for change, yet, at the same time takes into account the hold our cultural context has over us. Too radical a change is rarely proven to be a good idea. Long-term change needs gradual implementation, which is guided by the ultimate goal of happiness but is considerate to the context and requirements of the instigators of any such change.

I have then two aims: One is 'proactive' and the other is 'reactive'. The former being the bolder of the two, in that, it prescribes a genuine re-articulation of what a couple agrees to do in the first place, whilst the second and more modest hope is that monogamous couples become less arrogant in their assurances that they are "Right; period". However, it is a point in fact that the author would take no pleasure in other people's distress just to score a point for this theory. The secondary aim is, simply, to spell out the fragility of basing one's relationship – in terms of continuation – solely on fidelity. In this way the aim is reactive in the sense that with greater understanding, couples who opt for the absolutist path will hopefully be better equipped to manage their emotions and hence reactions when their dream is inevitably shattered.

It appears then, that before us lies a choice: (1) Keep the status quo, and chatter about value restoration. (2) Positively embrace serial monogamy as the modern manifestation of marriage. (3) Redefine what it is we agree to do in the first place in an attempt to restore life long partnerships to the ascendancy.

The first, whether an apocryphal story or not, sounds like the advice given to a Tudor monarch by a trusted aid who, when asked what to do in a time of crisis, replied "Do nothing it's far too serious".

The second implies that in affect we are changing the objective of longevity and should start introducing ourselves to our children as Mummy and Daddy but make sure they know that this is only the case (as far as a regular family goes), for as long as it lasts.

The third invites responsibility and pragmatism to adjust not the goal of our actions but the means of achieving it and is then in this sense my pro-active aim.

The "do nothing" approach (apart from lame appeals to pretending to live in the past) will of course only encourage and elaborate the appeal of serial monogamy. A society of serial monogamists is a society of people who cannot accept commitment to the value they hold most dear, namely that of monogamy. I am well aware of the fact that there are many other factors that have to be taken into account in order to have a comprehensive explanation of separation. However, attention to these is to concentrate on the details of emotional experience and that I leave to self-help books and social theorists. To pay attention to these in the support of monogamy is to duck the issue. It is like having a garden and constantly weeding and tending the flowerbeds but never cutting the lawn. You will never see the fruits of your toils from the kitchen window. As far as I am concerned, serial monogamy in the vast majority of cases is a product of that belief. The irony being we think we are being virtuous because we are not *fucking* anybody else and all the time we are *'fucking up'* the childhood of our children. The children have to cope with the reality that we cannot cope with as we, literally, throw the baby out with the bath water.

The change required to rescue us from the onset of serial monogamy is a dual shift of emphasis. Firstly, the emphasis of 'rightness' or 'virtue' needs to shift from monogamy to loyalty and therefore stability. As I have argued, how we feel about monogamy is in our control but how we act under its constraints is less so. Secondly, and most importantly the emphasis of trust must also shift from a brittle trust dependent on fidelity to a trust embedded in our partner's loyalty. In other words, the vow of faithfulness should be perceived in terms of loyalty and longevity allowing the liberation of the individual within the context of a single, life long relationship not at the expense of it. The vow then that should be taken in 'formal' marriage or assumed in 'informal' marriage should be something along the lines of "I promise to be loyal to you but faithful to myself". In this way, we will more likely promise what can be delivered and ground relationships on *what we are* and not *"wouldn't it be nice if this were who we were?"*

The promised fidelity of our partner is difficult to sacrifice. This is not easy. But the fact remains, that all those who have been unfaithful know that we are more than capable of doing so without it changing how we feel about our partners. So, why outside of selfishness is it not possible to afford our partners the same respect? Greater self-confidence and fettering of our jealousy would facilitate a more proportioned response when our partners fall foul of the pressures outlined in this essay.

Perhaps, it would help to think of our present condition in terms of a terminal illness. The vaccine is for us to invent and, therefore, the cure lies in the future and that is for our future children. However, like all other illnesses we must take the medicine to keep us alive and for the present, that medicine must be the continued use of deception. Still operating on the principle of "what we don't know won't hurt us" but with a crucial difference. That difference being, that it is premised on *discovery*. At the moment we agree with or, at least, acquiesce in the expectation of fidelity so when we are unfaithful the deception is based on the fact that it is imperative that we are not caught. So the deception is seen as devious, dishonest and selfish, thus entailing the wrath and condemnation that these adjectives attract. Also built into this system is a partners right to ask, which can only exacerbate the lying and deceiving. However, with re-articulation, and the grounding of virtue and trust in loyalty, running parallel with an acceptance of romance as a separate state, fidelity is never agreed to, when undertaking the life commitment. Therefore, there is no promise to be broken. This being the case, deception is merely a consideration to the unhealthy state of mind that history has left us with and should then be seen in terms of a 'white lie'. In short, the difference being we deceive to do what we have agreed to do instead of deceiving to do what we have not agreed to do. In turn, if one wishes to swallow the medicine of deception then it is in one's interests not to ask questions or snoop on our partners. Nonetheless, if indiscretions are discovered they should be met with the appropriate disapproval that accompanies a white lie, as the lie was for the benefit of the one lied to and not the liar, and in the knowledge that the liar has not lied, to break a promise.

The huge over-reaction, which is commonplace as things presently stand, must be transcended, if we are to avoid the social menace and dishonesty that serial monogamy personifies. Serial monogamy is not just negative for the children it is also a negative overall life experience for the parent as it is, essentially, the enactment of repetition as opposed to progression. More or less the same experience lived two, three or how many times. A little respite of "Just met", before the same old problems start to appear on the horizon. To condense the sentiment of this book in one sentence I quote Rochefoucauld's luminous maxim 'We promise according to our hopes and perform according to our fears'. The task now then is to start performing to our hopes by confronting and conquering our fears.

CPSIA information can be obtained at www.ICGtesting.com
Printed in the USA
LVOW12s0416240514

386972LV00010B/72/P